CISTERCIAN FATHERS SERIES: NUMBER EIGHTY-FOUR

Bernard of Clairvaux

VARIOUS SERMONS

CISTERCIAN FATHERS SERIES: NUMBER EIGHTY-FOUR

Bernard of Clairvaux

Various Sermons

Translated by
Grace Remington, OCSO

Introduction by
Alice Chapman

Cistercian Publications
www.cistercianpublications.org

LITURGICAL PRESS
Collegeville, Minnesota
www.litpress.org

A Cistercian Publications title published by Liturgical Press

Cistercian Publications
Editorial Offices
161 Grosvenor Street
Athens, Ohio 45701
www.cistercianpublications.org

The translations of sermons 1–9 are based on the *Sermons de varii*, in Jean Leclercq and H. M. Rochais, *Sancti Bernardi Opera* (Rome: Editiones Cistercienses, 1970), 6/1:9–55. The translation of sermon 10 is based on the Latin text edited by Gaetano Raciti, in Saint Bernard de Clairvaux, *Sermons variés*, Sources Chrétiennes 526 (Paris: Les Éditions du Cerf, 2010), 174–98. The translation of *The Life of Saint Victor* is based on the *Acta Sanctorum Bollandia*, Feb. III (Paris, 1865), 671–72.

Scripture texts in this work are translated by the translator of the sermons.

1 2 3 4 5 6 7 8 9

Library of Congress Cataloging-in-Publication Data

Names: Bernard, of Clairvaux, Saint, 1090 or 1091-1153, author. | Remington, Grace, translator.
Title: Various sermons / Bernard of Clairvaux ; translated by Grace Remington, OCSO ; introduction by Alice Chapman.
Other titles: Sermons. Selections. English
Description: Collegeville, Minnesota : Cistercian Publications, 2020. | Series: Cistercian fathers; number eighty-four | Includes index. | Summary: "A loose assemblage of sermons outside of the organized collections of Bernard's sermons treating themes of the life of desire, the true meaning of holiness, and the awakening of the spiritual senses in the search for God"— Provided by publisher.
Identifiers: LCCN 2019045386 (print) | LCCN 2019045387 (ebook) | ISBN 9780879071844 (paperback) | ISBN 9780879075842 (epub) | ISBN 9780879075842 (mobi) | ISBN 9780879075842 (pdf)
Subjects: LCSH: Catholic Church—Sermons. | Sermons, Latin—Translations into English.
Classification: LCC BX891.3 .B4713 2020 (print) | LCC BX891.3 (ebook) | DDC 252/.02—dc23
LC record available at https://lccn.loc.gov/2019045386
LC ebook record available at https://lccn.loc.gov/2019045387

Contents

Acknowledgments

I AM GRATEFUL to Stefano Mula, Lewis White, Dom Elias Dietz, and Fr. Michael Casey for their generous assistance in answering questions I had concerning this translation. I am especially grateful to Marsha Dutton for her close reading of this text through several variations, and without whose advice and insight this translation would not have been possible. In addition, I am indebted to the kindness and good zeal of my Latin professor at Grinnell College, Ed Phillips, who repeatedly rearranged his schedule to accommodate a biology major who wanted to take advanced Latin, and who taught the language with passion, patience, and skill.

Abbreviations

CCCM	Corpus Christianorum, Continuatio Mediaevalis
CDH	Anselm, *Cur Deus Homo?*
CF	Cistercian Fathers series (Cistercian Publications)
Coll	*Collectanea Cisterciensis*
CS	Cistercian Studies series (Cistercian Publications)
CSQ	*Cistercian Studies Quarterly*
RB	Rule of St. Benedict
PL	Patrologia Latina
SBOp	Sancti Bernardi Opera
SCh	Sources Chrétiennes
VSV	The Life of St. Victor

Bernard's Works

Ann	Sermo in annuntiatione domini
BenV	Sermo in natali Sancti Benedicti (=VLH)
Csi	*De Consideratione*
Dil	*Liber de diligendo Deo*
Div	Sermo de diversis
Ep(p	Epistle(s
Gra	*Liber de gratia et libero arbitrio*
MalE	*Epitaphium sancti Malachiæ*
MalH	Hymnus de sancto Malachiæ
MalS	Sermo de sancto Malachiæ
MalT	Sermo in transitu sancti Malachiæ episcopi (=VLH)
MalV	*Vita sancti Malachiæ*
OS	Sermo in festivitate Omnium Sanctorum
Pasc	Sermo in die paschæ
Pre	*Liber de præcepto et dispensatione*
SC	Sermo super Cantica canticorum

SSV	Sermo de sancto Victori
VLH	Verba lectionis huius (=S Ben V)

Introduction to Bernard of Clairvaux's Various Sermons (*Sermones varii*)

Alice Chapman

BERNARD OF CLAIRVAUX (d. 1153) was a pivotal figure in the history of the Cistercian Order, and his sermons are some of the most influential and significant of the Middle Ages.[1] His sermon collections exemplify an eloquence and proficiency unmatched in Western Christendom.[2] Through his command of language and imagery, Bernard called his monks to engage in continual and daily conversion in the ongoing monastic quest toward conversion of life (*conversatio morum*).[3] But his preaching reached beyond the cloister into

[1] As an entry point into Bernard of Clairvaux's life and significance, see Brian Patrick McGuire, ed., *A Companion to Bernard of Clairvaux*, Brill's Companions to the Christian Tradition, vol. 25 (Leiden and Boston: Brill, 2011). Also see Martha G. Newman, *The Boundaries of Charity: Cistercian Culture and Ecclesiastical Reform, 1098–1180* (Stanford: Stanford University Press, 1996); and Jean Leclercq, *The Love of Learning and the Desire for God: A Study of Monastic Culture*, trans. Catherine Misrahi, 2nd ed. (New York: Fordham University Press, 1992).

[2] Wim Verbaal, "The Preaching of Community: Bernard of Clairvaux's Sermons and the School of Experience," *Medieval Sermon Studies* 48 (2004): 75–90. Also see Verbaal's Introduction to Bernard of Clairvaux, *Sermons for the Autumn Season*, trans. Irene Edmonds, CF 54 (Collegeville, MN: Cistercian Publications, 2016), ix–lxvi, and his Introduction to Bernard of Clairvaux, *Sermons for Lent and the Easter Season*, trans. Irene Edmonds, et al., CF 52 (Kalamazoo, MI: Cistercian Publications, 2007), vii–lix. See also Jean Leclercq, "Sur le caractère littéraire des sermons de saint Bernard," *Studi medievali* 7 (1966): 701–44; Mette Birkedal Bruun, *Parables: Bernard of Clairvaux's Mapping of Spiritual Topography* (Leiden and New York: Brill, 2007).

[3] RB 58.17: *Suscipiendus autem in oratorio coram omnibus promittat de stabilitate sua et conversatione morum suorum et oboedientia.* "Let the one being received promise before all in the oratory stability, conversion of life, and obedience."

the church. His "On Conversion: a Sermon to Clerics" and "Sermon on Saint Malachy" can be read with his treatise *On Consideration: Advice to a Pope* as painting a vivid picture of excellent ecclesiastical leadership, rooted in humility and focused on ministry following the example of Christ. Among his most famous and possibly most beautiful sermons, the Sermons on the Song of Songs lift the eyes of the reader to spiritual heights in contemplation of God, allowing the soul to glimpse the ultimate unity of the soul with God. Bernard's over five hundred letters reveal his connection with and involvement in the most important ecclesiastical, spiritual, and political issues of his day.[4] Of the 8 volumes of Sancti Bernardi Opera (SBOp), the Latin edition of his works published by Jean Leclercq, H. M. Rochais, and C. H. Talbot between 1957 and 1977, sermons fill 5, adding up to a staggering 729 sermons.[5]

There are ten sermons in the current collection. Leclercq gathered nine of them and placed them together in SBOp volume 6/1, titling them *Sermones varii*, or *Various Sermons*.[6] This collection should not be confused with the *Sermons on Diverse Topics*, the *De diversis*, which are primarily monastic sermons and reflect Bernard's preaching style.[7]

[4] Much of Bernard's involvement in the debates and issues of his day can be found among his letters. For the most recent dating and discussion of Bernard's collected letters, see the *Opere di San Bernardo*, ed. Ferruccio Gastaldelli (Milan: Scriptorium Claravallense, Fondazione di Studi Cisterciensi, 1984, 1986), 6:1–2. For the English version, which includes Gastaldelli's updates, see the 1998 reprint version of *The Letters of St Bernard of Clairvaux*, trans. Bruno Scott James (Stroud, UK: Sutton Publishing, 1998), 531–37, 538–52.

[5] This number has been calculated by Michael Casey; see his introduction to Bernard of Clairvaux's *Monastic Sermons*, CF 86 (Collegeville, MN: Cistercian Publications, 2016), xiv, n. 4.

[6] *Sancti Bernardi Opera*, ed. Jean Leclercq and Henri-Marie Rochais (Rome: Editiones Cistercienses, 1970), 6/1:9–55.

[7] For a good assessment of the oral style of the *De diversi* sermons, see Jean Leclercq's Introduction, *Sermoni diversi e vari*, Opere di San Bernardo 4 (Milan: Scriptorium claravallense, Fondazione di studi Cisterciensi, 2000), 3–25. It is also available in English, "Introduction to Saint Bernard's *Sermones varii*," trans. Elias Dietz, CSQ 43, no. 2 (2008): 147–60. For a comparison of Bernard's literary style and preaching style, see Jean Leclercq, "Were the Sermons on the Song of Songs Delivered in Chapter?," Introduction, *Sermons on the Song of Songs II*, trans. Kilian Walsh, CF 7 (Kalamazoo, MI: Cistercian Publications, 1983), vii–xxx, esp. xiii–xxiv. See also Chris-

Leclercq placed the nine *De varii* sermons under eight headings, with the two sermons on the Feast of Saint Victor together under one entry. As the name of the collection suggests, no thematic or cohesive idea unites the sermons. In addition to the nine sermons in the Latin edition, Gaetano Raciti has discovered one other sermon, included here under the title "For the Feast of Saint Benedict."[8] Leclercq arranged these sermons roughly chronologically, according to the liturgical year. Although the sermon "For the Feast of Saint Benedict" would thus fit liturgically after the two sermons for the feast of Saint Victor, in this volume it comes at the end of the collection.

One of Bernard's greatest achievements is the sermon collection for the liturgical year (*Sermones per annum*) in SBOp volumes 4–5 (SBOp 4:117–496, 5:1–451). Over a period of years, Bernard collected, revised, and edited this series of sermons.[9] As a result, they demonstrate literary excellence. Leclercq identified four successive versions of this collection, which he viewed as developing toward a "perfect" final version.[10] These four stages are often referred to by a letter, signifying where they fall in their chronological development: B (*brevis*), between 1138–1140; M (*media*), ca. 1140; L (*longior*), after 1148, and Pf (*perfecta*), complete before 1153. Wim Verbaal's groundbreaking work has revolutionized our understanding of Bernard's liturgical sermons. Verbaal has shown that the four stages of development are not a chronological succession aiming at a perfect version. Rather, each part has its own emphasis and character. For example, the sermons in B have a moral quality and focus on the "liberation of the human soul" while M and Pf focus on the liturgical year. The largest collection, L, seems to be

---

topher Holdsworth, "Were the Sermons of St. Bernard on the Song of Songs ever Preached?" *Medieval Monastic Preaching* (Leiden: Brill, 1998), 295–318.

[8] See the introduction and text for this sermon in Bernard de Clairvaux, *Sermons variés*, ed. Françoise Callerot, Pierre-Yves Emery, and Gaetano Raciti, Œuvres completes XXVIII B, SCh 526 (Paris: Les Éditions du Cerf, 2010), 161–72.

[9] See Verbaal's Introduction, CF 54:ix–xiii. For Bernard as a writer, see M. B. Pranger, "Bernard the Writer," in *A Companion to Bernard of Clairvaux*, ed. Brian Patrick McGuire (Leiden and Boston: Brill, 2011), 220–48.

[10] See SBOp 4:ix–xvii, 130–31; pages 130–31 contain a helpful chart of the sermons included in each redaction of the collection. For a more complete assessment of the collection, see Jean Leclercq, "La tradition des sermons liturgiques de S. Bernard," in *Recueil d'études sur saint Bernard et ses écrits* (Rome: Storia et Letteratura, 1966), 2:203–60.

an independent, parallel collection with two distinct halves. Verbaal's insights have revealed a deeper complexity and intentionality about the way Bernard organized his sermons; in so doing he has provided a glimpse into Bernard himself.[11]

Because some of the texts in the *Various Sermons* resemble the liturgical sermons, many scholars view them as an extension or appendix to the sermons for the liturgical year.[12] But Leclercq grouped and titled them separately, because Bernard had not selected them for inclusion among the liturgical collection (SBOp 6/1:3–6).

Authenticity

In addition to the carefully edited liturgical series, Bernard also wrote a variety of other sermons. Some were short sermon outlines, like those in the *Sentences*, and still others reflect his monastic preaching, like the *Sermons on Diverse Topics*.[13] At times, Bernard simply dictated a sermon outline, and at other times he may have worked with a secretary. Leclercq observes, "some of the texts that are clearly Saint Bernard's are not his in the same way, depending on whether they were drawn up by Bernard alone, or by Bernard and a secretary, or only by a secretary."[14] As a result, it is impossible to determine the Bernardine authenticity of a text on the basis of its phrasing or style, both of which varied according to context and genre.[15] The work of

[11] Wim Verbaal, Introduction, CF 54:ix. Also see Wim Verbaal, Introduction to Bernard of Clairvaux, *Sermons for Advent and the Christmas Season*, trans. Irene Edmonds, et al., CF 51 (Kalamazoo, MI: Cistercian Publications, 2007), vii–lix; and Wim Verbaal, Introduction, CF 52:vii–lxiii.

[12] Raciti made this observation twice in *Sermons variés*: SCh 526:22, 161.

[13] See Casey, Introduction, CF 8:xv.

[14] Leclercq, "Introduction to *Sermones varii*," 147.

[15] Jeroen De Gussem encourages readers and scholars to think differently about medieval authorship. Challenging the assumptions of both Leclercq and Rochais, De Gussem focuses on "computational stylistics" to distinguish authorship in evaluating the work of Bernard of Clairvaux and his most famous secretary, Nicholas of Montiéramey. De Gussem argues for "turns of phrase that reveal [Nicholas's] presence." The comparison of clusters of phrases specific to each author, he says, does not establish a "hierarchical 'author-scribe' relationship," but rather challenges one to realize

determining authenticity needs different criteria. The veracity of the ten texts in this collection has been established using both internal and external evidence. The internal evidence consists of evaluation of the ideas and their mode of progression throughout the text, whereas the external evidence is determined by the manuscript tradition.[16] The "Context" section of the introduction for each sermon briefly addresses and discusses its authenticity.

In the *Sermones varii*, the first two sermons follow the liturgical year, with the first for the season of Advent, "For Advent: On the Three Realms of the Dead" (AdvV), and the second for Epiphany, "For Epiphany" (EpiV). Four sermons are associated with saints' days, appearing here as they appear in the liturgical cycle: "For the Conversion of Saint Paul" (PlV), the "First [and Second] Sermons for the Feast of Saint Victor" (VicS1, VicS2), and one "For the Feast of Saint Benedict" (BenV). The remaining four sermons fall outside the liturgical cycle and reflect spiritual or theological themes. These include "On the Will of God" (Vol) and "On the Mercies of the Lord" (Mise), "On The Seven Gifts of the Holy Spirit" (Doni), and one in honor of the great Irish saint, Malachy, archbishop of Armagh, "On Saint Malachy" (MalS).[17] With the exception of the two sermons for the Feast of Saint Victor, which could not have been written before 1137, and the sermon "On Saint Malachy," dating after 1148, there is no secure date for the sermons.[18]

This English version of the *Various Sermons* is based on the critical edition by Leclercq and H. M. Rochais.[19] It remains the standard Latin version of Bernard's texts used today. An earlier version of Bernard's

that "the practice of cooperative medieval authorship is complex, and . . . medieval authorship is interminably diffuse" ("Bernard of Clairvaux and Nicholas of Montiéramey: Tracing the Secretarial Trail with Computational Stylistics," *Speculum* 92, no. S1 [October 2017]: S190–S225, here S215).

16 Leclercq, "Introduction to *Sermones varii*," 147–49.

17 Gaetano Raciti, "Un nouveau sermon de saint Bernard – *Verba lectionis huius* – pour la fête de Saint Benoît," Coll 60 (1998): 60–107.

18 *Bernhard von Clairvaux: Sämtliche Werke*, ed. Gerhard B. Winkler, Band 9 (Innsbruck, Austria: Tyrolia Verlag, 1997), 29–30.

19 *Sancti Bernardi Opera*, ed. Jean Leclercq and Henri-Marie Rochais, 8 vols in 9 (Rome: Editiones Cistercienses, 1957–1977).

sermons was compiled in the seventeenth century by Jean Mabillon.[20] Although Mabillon had published six of these in his volume of Bernard's works, they did not belong to the liturgical series, and Leclercq removed them from the collection of liturgical sermons and placed them in the *De varii* collection in SBOp. To these six, Leclercq added three others, previously unpublished, one for Advent, one for Epiphany, and "On the Seven Gifts of the Holy Spirit." The tenth sermon of the English translation below, "For the Feast of Saint Benedict" was not part of the nine in *De varii*.

Mabillon's edition was the basis for volume 183 of the Patrologia Latina, edited by Jacques-Paul Migne and published in 1854. Ailbe Luddy prepared an English translation of the sermons from this Latin edition in 1921, but because it followed the Mabillon edition it contained only six of the nine sermons contained in SBOp.[21] This new English version includes all nine sermons in the SBOp, plus a tenth sermon, "For the Feast of Benedict." This fresh and readable translation allows for broader readership, and for Saint Bernard's sermons to reach an even wider audience.

Sermon One: For Advent: On the Three Realms of the Dead

Context

This first sermon, often referred to as "In Celebration of Advent," is associated with the beginning of the liturgical year.[22] Although Bernard wrote many sermons for Advent, he did not include this sermon with the other seven, which he included in his sermons for the liturgical year.[23] The text was, however, known to scholars and to

[20] Jean Mabillon, *Sancti Bernardi abbatis Clarae-Vallensis Opera Omnia* (Paris: Gaume, 1839).

[21] *St. Bernard's Sermons for the Seasons and Principal Festivals of the Year*, trans. Ailbe Luddy, 3 vols. (Westminster, MD: Carroll Press, 1950).

[22] This title is taken from the first few words of the sermon, "In celebratione adventus Domini," SBOp 6/1:9.

[23] There are seven Advent sermons in the liturgical series of Bernard's sermons; see SBOp 5:161–96. For an assessment of their content and context, see Verbaal's introduction to CF 51:vii–lxii.

Mabillon, who knew the text and had an annotated copy. Since the style seemed different from that of Bernard's other sermons, Mabillon questioned its authenticity. He was apparently convinced by the annotator's gloss that the content of the sermon reflected a "more eloquent and less sacred" style than that which characterized Bernard's sermons.[24] The sermon lingered in relative obscurity and remained unpublished until 1951, when a version appeared in the Cistercian journal *Collectanea Cisterciensia*.[25] Its wider distribution, however, did not occur until it was included in SBOp's 1970 volume of *Sermones varii* (SBOp 6/1:9–55).

The issues of style that caused Mabillon's suspicions about the veracity of this text are readily apparent, but Leclercq dismissed the assessment as "vague" and considered the sermon genuine. The overall style is certainly different from that of many of Bernard's other sermons, but it is possible that it was the work of a secretary, as would account for the difference. Leclercq addressed this question in detail, arguing that external (manuscript transmission) and internal (ideas and vocabulary) evidence proved the authenticity of the text.[26] Since the publication of SBOp, this sermon has been accepted as a genuine work of Bernard and has subsequently been included in the German (1998), Italian (2000), and French (2010) collections. It is likewise accepted as genuine here.[27]

[24] The French version of Bernard's sermons was edited by Françoise Callerot, Pierre-Yves Emery, and Gaetano Raciti. See Raciti's remarks about Mabillon's perception of this sermon in SCh 526:36. Mabillon's copy of the sermon was annotated by Dom Saint-Beuve, who raised two major issues about the sermon's authenticity: "[it was] more eloquent and less sacred" than most of Bernard's sermons, and the "many divisions" do not reflect Bernard's manner (see Jean Leclercq, "L'àuthenticité Bernadine du sermon in celebratione adventus," *Recueil d'études*, 2:271).

[25] Gaetano Raciti, "Un Sermon inédit de saint Bernard pour l'Avent," Coll 13 (1951): 283–94.

[26] For a discussion of "authenticity," see Leclercq, "Introduction to *Sermones varii*," 147–60. Also see Leclercq, "L'àuthenticité Bernadine," 271–90.

[27] Winkler, *Bernhard von Clairvaux, Sämtliche Werke*; *San Bernardo: Sermoni diversi e vari*, in *Opere di San Bernardo*, ed. Ferruccio Gastaldelli, vol. 4 (Milan: Scriptorium Claravallense, Fondazione di Studi Cistercensi, 2008); Bernard de Clairvaux, *Sermons variés*, SCh 526.

Content

The first part of this Advent sermon focuses on the consequences of original sin and sets up three categories of people according to their different reactions to their common condition. Adam's sin, Bernard writes, cast all of humanity into a prison in which there are "three realms of the dead" (*triplex siquidem est infernus*). But the phrase "three realms of the dead" is deceptive, because the categories apply to the living rather than to the dead. As the sermon sometimes slides from a discussion of the present to the consequences of sin at the end of life, the reader must be alert to these shifts.[28]

Another issue that confronts the reader is vocabulary. The Latin term *infernus* can mean "hell" in the sense of the condition of the damned, but it has a range of meanings, for example "netherworld" or "purgatory"; in this volume the translation varies according to the Latin context (see p. 3, n. 1). Other terms are less flexible, as is the case with the Latin term *culpa*,[29] which denotes culpability and is commonly translated into English as *fault*.

Bernard divides the world into three parts, the "netherworld of destruction" (*infernus consumptionis*), where there is no redemption, the "netherworld of expiation" (*infernus expiationis*), in which souls are purged of sin (*purgandis*), and the "netherworld of the afflicted" (*infernus afflictionis*), for those who will not face Judgment but pass into everlasting life. Those in the second category must go through a process of purification, of purgation. The result of this process is the remission of the punishment (*poena*) of sin but not the fault (*culpa*). This text has been interpreted as a statement about the eschatological reality of the afterlife, in which there is a "lower" and an "intermediate" hell.[30]

[28] "In celebratione adventus Domini" (also called "De triplici inferno"), SBOp 6/1:11.

[29] This is translated as *guilt* in the English below. The German translation translates *culpa* as *die Schuld*, and the French as *la faute*.

[30] This text is cited and discussed in chapter four of Jacques Le Goff's book, *The Birth of Purgatory* (Chicago: University of Chicago Press, 1986). Le Goff interprets this sermon as a description of the afterlife; see his interpretation of the sermon on pages 145–46. He incorrectly designates the sermon as "the third sermon for Advent," but it is actually this sermon from *De varii*. The number 3 in question refers to the paragraph where this passage appears.

However, Bernard is describing three realms of the dead on earth since the Fall. This does not seem to be a conscious doctrinal statement but rather may reflect what Raciti calls a "tone of teaching."[31]

Those in Bernard's third category are those in monastic life, who undertake "voluntary poverty" (*paupertas voluntaria*) by renouncing the world and selfish desires and undertaking penance and seeking spiritual perfection.[32] Monks voluntarily embrace penance and live lives in pursuit of spiritual purity; they will pass into life rather than experience Judgment. But those who do not take on this kind of life and continue living according to the flesh may find that they may descend into one of the other two realms after death.

As they have committed themselves to a life of poverty and penance, God offers those in this category "the cup," which represents God's grace, the power to save. But the content of the cup differs according to who drinks from it. Some taste "pure wine" (*vinum merum*), because they embrace self-denial, taking on the passion of Christ by picking up the cross and following him (Matt 16:24). Others, however, taste "mixed wine" (*vinum mixtum*), because they are holding on to the cares and worries of the world. Still others drink the "dregs" (*faex*) and partake of the "cup of pestilence and not the cup of salvation," because they are caught in the throes of the flesh and do not call on the name of the Lord (Ps 115:13).

Halfway through the sermon, the focus turns toward the description of the monastic life, that is, the monastic church explained with an allusion to Augustine's City of God. Now Bernard identifies the monks as in the "netherworld of poverty," those who come together to form the beautiful and holy city of God, despite the fact that they remain in the midst of earthly affliction.[33] The earthly city is the Bridegroom's Beloved, the church, specifically the monastery. Invoking a passage

[31] "En réalité, le ton est celui d'un enseignement qui, certes, ne fait pas l'impasse sur la dureté et les risques de la condition humaine, provenant du péché d'Adam" (SCh 526:34). Thus he notes that even while writing as a teacher Bernard does not ignore the difficulties and risks of the human condition because of Adam's sin.

[32] Bernard discusses monastic poverty in S 77 *De diversis* (SBOp 6/1:317).

[33] SBOp 6/1:14. On the Bridegroom and the city of God, see Bernard, SC 32, 68, and 72 (SBOp 1:228; 2:199, 229). For the English, see *Sermons on the Song of Songs* II and IV, trans. Kilian Walsh and Irene Edmonds, respectively (Kalamazoo, MI: Cistercian Publications, 1976, 1980), CF 4:134–43; CF 40:17–25; 62–74.

from the Song of Songs, Bernard says that the beloved is as beautiful and sweet as Jerusalem, but also as fearsome and terrible as troops arrayed for battle (*castrorum acies ordinate*). His metaphors are spiritual but expressed in military terms: repentance (*paenitentia*) draws the troops together, vigilance (*vigilantia*) provides the arms, and "a union of hearts furnishes unanimity [*consensum*]" (SBOp 6/1:14). This is the allegorical image of the Church, who sojourns on Earth with her Bridegroom but who must wait for the final consummation until they meet in heaven.[34]

Defended by its spiritual troops, unity torments the enemy, and the devil is terrified not of fasting or continence but of love. The allegorical city, based on the Song of Songs 4:4, describes the neck of the bride as like "a tower of David, built with battlements. A thousand shields hang from it." This tower gathers virtues together and connects the head to the body. The tower belongs to David, who prefigures Christ here, both the Head and the one who gives himself up to redeem the world. The love between people reflects a heavenly love, and love itself is the "firm and unshakable city." The city is built on a foundation of humility, and the walls are made of obedience, which require patience to endure. Monastic themes and references abound, and obedience, humility, prayer, faith, vigilance, and justice band together to build and defend the city.[35] This is the city in which peace can flourish, a haven from the turmoil and confusion that abound in Babylon, a metaphor for the world.

Bernard presents all of this material as preparation for the Gospel of peace, which must be proclaimed to others. In order to do so, he instructs, "we must put shoes on the feet of our thoughts," that is, judge oneself harshly but demonstrate mercy toward one's neighbor (SBOp 6/1:17). In the end, all of the spiritual effort is designed to prepare the soil to receive the mustard seed and allow it to grow. The journey is arduous, but light awaits ahead. This is Bernard's message for Advent: prepare now for the glory to come.

[34] See sermon 86, the final sermon in the *Sermons on the Song of Songs*, SBOp 2:317–20.

[35] Monastic justice is expressed by an example from the Rule of Benedict Prol. 49 as giving "to each what belongs to them: obedience to seniors, instruction to juniors, cheerfulness to friends, and patience to enemies" (SBOp 6/1:17).

Sermon Two: For Epiphany

Context

The arrival of the magi on Epiphany, traditionally celebrated on January 6, marks the first recognition of Jesus' divinity. The very meaning of the word, "appearance from above," conveys its importance in the Christian year. Because it was a significant feast, Cistercians celebrated it for eight days, an octave. Therefore Bernard composed sermons not only for the Feast of Epiphany itself but also for the octave and the Sunday that followed.[36] Since this Epiphany sermon was not among those that Bernard collected and edited for the liturgical year, Mabillon did not include it in his seventeenth-century collection. It thus remained unpublished until it was included among the *Sermones varii* in the 1970 SBOp edition (SBOp 6/1:10–55).

Although this Epiphany sermon was not included in Bernard's series of liturgical sermons, its authenticity is not in question, since both the manuscript tradition and the consistency of the content have been established (SBOp 6/1:3–4). This sermon was part of a manuscript transmission associated with the Cistercian house of Morimond; Leclercq says, "it is there that the oldest texts are found."[37] In a sense, this sermon departs from the more careful style of Bernard's more literary sermons, and the language is at certain points imprecise. Its ideas appear in a rather disjointed way, in what Raciti has called "leaps of thought," evident throughout the text.[38] Both the content and the ideas contained in the sermon also reflect its authenticity, and some of the prominent themes are consistent with other works of Bernard.

[36] In his *Sermons for the Liturgical Year*, Bernard included three sermons for Epiphany, one on the octave, and two for the Sunday after the octave of Epiphany. See SBOp 4:291–326, and the English version, under the title, *Sermons for Advent and the Christmas Season*, trans. Irene Edmonds, et al., CF 51 (Kalamazoo, MI: Cistercian Publications, 2007), 154–93.

[37] Leclercq, "Introduction to Saint Bernard's *Sermones varii*," 151. In SBOp 6/1:3–4, Leclercq lists the manuscripts and explains the manuscript transmission of the sermon, demonstrating the association of the texts with the "zone de Morimond" or the "area of Morimond." This analysis establishes the external evidence for the authenticity of the sermon.

[38] Raciti, *Sermons variés*, SCh 526:81. Raciti also acknowledges some clumsiness in the writing.

Content

The sermon opens with a brief overview outlining the three reasons for the feast: it marks the arrival of the magi, celebrates the baptism of Jesus, and commemorates the changing of the water into wine at John the Evangelist's wedding at Cana. After this brief introduction, it makes a dramatic turn toward an assessment of the "moral teaching" of the feast's mysteries.[39] Three things, Bernard says, are necessary for the soul to return "home" (*ad patriam*): "the will, the ability, and the knowledge" (*velle, posse, nosse*).[40] Reason (*ratio*), guided by grace, makes judgments to which the will gives assent, and then the body carries out the action in loyal service. But the devil interrupts proper order, confusing reason with deceit, perverting the desire of the will, and causing the flesh to be occupied with carousing. The result is a fundamental disorder, elevating the will over reason, which is now a captive, leaving the flesh to obey an errant will.

In addition to sowing discord, the devil aims to trap humanity in a morass of sin, resulting in "being unable to avoid sin."[41] Bernard had earlier similarly addressed sin and the human will in *On Grace and Free Will* (Gra),[42] which provides the conceptual backdrop here, explaining

[39] For medieval writers, the biblical text had different levels of meaning, the literal, allegorical, moral (or tropological), and spiritual (or anagogical). The literal meaning takes the text at face value, focusing on its obvious meaning, while the allegorical sought to probe a deeper meaning. For Bernard, this pattern often meant reading the text as in light of the allegorical relationship between Christ and the Church. The moral or tropological reading understood the text as conveying a lesson or some kind of moral instruction, while the spiritual meaning sought to plumb the depths of meaning in relation of the soul to God. This was the highest meaning, reserved for the spiritually advanced. See Bernard McGinn, *The Growth of Mysticism*, vol. 2 of *The Presence of God: A History of Western Christian Mysticism* (New York: Crossroad, 1994), 40–41.

[40] For the concept of the soul's return to its homeland (*patria*), see Bernard, *On Grace and Free Will* (SBOp 3:171), *Apology* (SBOp 3:183), and *Sentences* (SBOp 6/2:252).

[41] Cf. Augustine's *De correptione et gratia* 12.3 (PL 44:936); it is among Augustine's Anti-Pelagian writings. The English is *On Rebuke and Grace*, in Nicene and Post-Nicene Fathers Series I, 5:485.

[42] Freedom of choice (*liberum arbitrium*) is Bernard's focus in on *Grace and Free Choice*. This aspect of freedom was not lost in the Fall and will not be lost in heaven.

that Adam's decision to disobey God led to humanity's enslavement to sin. The result was the loss of two conditions: the inability to sin (*non posse peccare*) and the ability not to sin (*posse non peccare*), both of which were replaced by the inability to avoid sin, or not being able not to sin (*non posse non peccare*).[43] The only way to escape the bondage of sin, Bernard explains, is through the action of grace, which restores men and women (but only partially) to Adam's original condition, the ability not to sin (*posse non peccare*). Alone, humanity could not make satisfaction for the debt of sin. Making satisfaction was only possible if a "worthy payment" could be made, and only one person could pay the penalty for sin. Christ therefore had to make "proper satisfaction" for the debt incurred by humanity.[44]

This argument lies behind Bernard's discussion of sin in the Epiphany sermon. In paragraph three, Bernard explains its implications for his monks. The devil, he says, emphasizes only the painful aspects of

---

It is essential to the human condition. However, because of the Fall, human choice, although free, is exercised in a world ruled by sin. In that sense, it is free but exists in a condition of bondage. For the role of grace, see Gra 16; cf. Gra 4:10.

[43] Bernard explains that human beings have lost two of the three freedoms they possessed before the Fall. Freedom from sin, also called freedom of counsel (*liberum consilium*), has two parts, a superior and an inferior. The superior is the inability to sin (*non posse peccare*), and the inferior is the ability not to sin (*posse non peccare*). Although both parts are lost, action of grace can restore the inferior portion and is also progressive, increasing gradually over time. However, the superior part can only be restored in the celestial realm after death. Freedom from sorrow, which he refers to as freedom of pleasure (*liberum complacitum*), is also lost and can be regained only upon return to our homeland (*patria*), but by following the example of Mary and through contemplation, one can see a glimmer of happiness in this life, though rare and fleeting (SBOp 3:177). Freedom from necessity, that is, free choice (*liberum arbitrium*), continues to retain its innate freedom, since it is essential to humanity. The major difference since the Fall is that although freedom from necessity is mired in sin, this reality does not itself force or compel the will. Free choice remains free; its liberty is never lost (SBOp 3:169, 170, 177). Bernard maintains a radical freedom of the Will (*voluntas*), which he defines as a "self-determining habit of the soul" (SBOp 3:167).

[44] The similarities of Bernard's position to Anselm's argument in *Cur Deus Homo* (*Why God Became Man*) appear both here and again in Sermon Eight, "On the Seven Gifts of the Holy Spirit." I show the similarities to Anselm text together with some detailed analysis below in the introduction to that sermon. In particular, I consider the idea that humanity cannot pay the debt incurred at Fall and the terminology and idea of making "satisfaction" for the debt.

the rule (*ordinis tormenta*), stoking the fear of "future torments." The deception that follows is the human perception that the world is sweet and monastic life is bitter. The only remedy for this confusion, Bernard explains, is the action of grace, as the "Lord knocks at the door of the heart" in order to restore order, and reason cooperates and reemerges as the guide, commanding the body to open the door. When one thus opens the door to grace, "will screams in protest," as the flesh now acts contrary to the will, in cooperation with reason.

The Son of God brings peace to this internal conflict, reconciling humanity to God as Mediator and Redeemer. Bernard then re-envisions the gifts of the magi as offerings that each person—that is, each monk—should give to the Son, with reason bringing "the gold of devotion," the will "the incense of prayer," and the flesh "the myrrh of mortification." Each gift is proper to a different aspect of the Son; in order to conform to the "image of his humanity," in thanksgiving for his human suffering, one must present him with the gift of myrrh, which is the mortification of the flesh. In order to be "reformed" in the image of his divinity, one should offer the incense of prayer, following his example in this life so that through grace we might conform to his image in both body and spirit. Finally, in regard to his kingship, one ought to present the gold of devotion and acceptance of his leadership.

Once the gifts are presented, then one begins to know God and turns away from the world. The monk who has spent obedience to buy wisdom can now draw near to God and be enlightened according to Psalm 33:6. Having set aside the habits of the "old person," one can now walk in the light of the new according to the spirit. What comes is an inner peace, for where God is, there is joy, serenity, and happiness.

Sermon Three: For The Conversion of Saint Paul

Context

As the topic of this sermon is the most famous story of Christian conversion, it is no surprise that Bernard wrote two sermons for the occasion.[45] The sermon included here reflects Bernard's preaching style and is similar to the monastic sermons, *De diversis*. In fact, the sermon reads like a verbal meditation on a few words associated with conversion.[46]

Mabillon included this sermon as the second of two on the occasion of Paul's conversion and published it; its authenticity is well established, since it was part of several older manuscript collections. Leclercq has shown that this sermon was inserted in some manuscripts among the Pf collection, but since Bernard himself did not include it in his collection of liturgical sermons, the SBOp editors placed it among the *Sermones varii* (SBOp 6/1:4–5).

Content

The overall message of this sermon is that conversion is the key of the Christian life. Bernard clarifies the meaning of this idea at the beginning, saying that one must become like a child in order to enter the kingdom of heaven (Matt 18:3). This explanation is a play on Paul's name, which is connected to *parvulus*, the Latin word for a small child. The conversion of Paul, therefore, involves both his name and his heart, an external and internal conversion that Bernard calls a "double littleness" (SBOp 4:28). He treats a child as both the example of and model for conversion, but he does not mean that one must become childish. Rather, one must develop both interior littleness, humility, and exterior littleness, meekness.

In the second paragraph of this short sermon, Bernard focuses on the three ways Paul's conversion demonstrates meekness: by hurtful words, by the loss of something, and by bodily injury. He explains this process with the narrative of that conversion: first came the verbal

[45] The other sermon is among the liturgical sermons, SBOp 4:327–34. It also addresses conversion, but it is much longer and includes the narrative from Acts 9:4-5.

[46] Throughout the sermon, the Latin term for "converted," *conversus*, appears many times in various forms, including other related terms related to turning, such as *versus*, *aversus*, *adversus*, and *perversus*. Leclercq pointed out this play on words in his "Introduction to Saint Bernard's *Sermones varii*," 152.

confrontation, "Saul, Saul, why do you persecute me?" This was followed by a blow to the body, when Paul was knocked off his horse and thrown to the ground. Finally, he experienced the loss of his eyesight. Through all these trials, however, he persevered and showed patience; in so doing he demonstrated virtue, much as Job had done.

The final two sentences of this sermon explain why Bernard placed the emphasis on external rather than internal conversion. He explains that although his monks should have already experienced external conversion, some were still grumbling over physical injury or the loss of something, or, even worse, were resentful over hurtful words. For monks, the whole of one's life is conversion, and *conversatio morum*, a conversion of life, is an ongoing, daily process designed to help one grow closer to God.

Sermons Four and Five: Sermons For the Feast of Saint Victor

Context

The next two sermons are discussed together because they are both associated with the *Office of Saint Victor*. Bernard composed the office in honor of the sixth-century hermit Saint Victor of Arcies, after receiving a request from Abbot Guy of the Benedictine monastery at Montiéramey.[47] Abbot Guy asked Bernard to write an office for the feast of Saint Victor, whose remains had been translated to Montiéramey in 837. Bernard agreed, and as part of the office he wrote

[47] The connection between Abbot Guy and Bernard was Nicholas of Montiéramey, who was initially one of Bernard's trusted secretaries, but his penchant for plagiarism led to his expulsion from Clairvaux. For an assessment of issues related to authorship in Bernard's letters and sermons, see De Gussem, "Bernard of Clairvaux and Nicholas of Montiéramey," S204–225. Nicholas had been a member of the Benedictine house of Montiéramey before coming to Clairvaux (see Raciti, *Sermons variés*, SCh 526:119). This monastery was located close to the city of Troyes, in the Champagne region of France. For a detailed discussion of the *Office of Saint Victor*, see Jean Leclercq, "Saint Bernard Écrivain: d'après l'office de Saint Victor," *Revue Bénedictine* 74 (1964): 155–69. For an English version of a portion of this article, see Leclercq, "Introduction to *Sermones varii*," 152–55.

two sermons, which he instructed should be read as lessons at the monastic Office of Vigils.[48] Abbot Guy had sent Bernard the Life of Saint Victor, which served as a basis for the historical information contained in the Office.[49]

In a letter that accompanied the Office, Bernard provides clear evidence for the origin and authorship of the sermons: "I have written two sermons on the life of the saint in my own words but based upon the ancient accounts you sent me."[50] In addition to Bernard's letter, Leclercq has also provided a clear manuscript tradition for these two sermons; therefore, their authenticity is not in question.[51] Since these sermons were written specifically for the Office, they do not belong to the *Sermones per annum*; as a result, Leclercq has placed them in this series. Furthermore, the fact that the observance of the Feast of Saint Victor was not retained throughout the church strengthens the case for their placement here among the *Various Sermons*.[52]

Both the letter and the Office contain helpful material and are part of an historical picture that goes beyond their origin with Abbot Guy and Bernard. The "Office of Saint Victor" is part of a group of texts associated with the second reform of Cistercian liturgical practice, of which Bernard was an integral part. This reform dates to 1142–1147; three major Bernadine texts are associated with it: the "Prologue to the Cistercian Antiphonary," Letter 398, and the "Office of Saint Victor."[53]

[48] Guy became abbot in 1137; both sermons were written after that date. These sermons are included as Appendix 1 in Bernard de Clairvaux, *Office de Saint Victor, Prologue à L'Antiphonaire, Lettre 398*, ed. Claire Maître, et al., Oeuvres Complètes 30, SCh 527 (Paris: Les Éditions du Cerf, 2009), 201–10.

[49] See M. Basil Pennington's comments in the Introduction to "The Office of St Victor," in Bernard of Clairvaux, *Treatises I*, the Works of Bernard of Clairvaux, vol. 1, CF 1 (Shannon, Ireland: Cahill & Co., Ltd., 1970), 165–67.

[50] Ep 398 in SBOp 8:377–78; see the English translation, quoted here, from the 1998 reprint version of *The Letters of St Bernard of Clairvaux*, trans. Bruno Scott James (Stroud, UK: Sutton Publishing, 1998), 502.

[51] SBOp 6/1:5. Leclercq also specifies here that the two sermons are intended for the Office of Vigils.

[52] See Raciti's remarks, *Sermons variés*, SC 526:127.

[53] These three texts are often published together; for the English version, including introductions to each, see Chrysogonus Waddell, "Introduction to the Prologue to the Cistercian Antiphonary," and M. Basil Pennington, "Introduction to the Office

Content

THE FIRST SERMON FOR THE FEAST OF SAINT VICTOR

The "First Sermon for the Feast of Saint Victor" describes the life of the saint. Since Victor's name can be made into a kind of synonym for the Latin word *virtue* (*virtus*), Bernard spends a good deal of the first part of the sermon extolling his virtue, nine times in the first fifteen lines of the sermon. Virtue is a precondition for glory, he says; without it, glory is undeserved and "pursued prematurely." But exercised in the correct order, virtue can be a ladder to glory, one that leads to "glory rightfully owned and safely given."[54] Bernard bases this discussion on Psalm 88:18, a portion of which he includes in the first part of the sermon: "because you are the glory of their virtue." Since the Psalms form the scriptural basis of the monastic life, it is no surprise that several figure prominently in the sermon.

As one who possesses both virtue and glory, Victor should be admired and emulated. Following his example, Bernard encourages the monks to strive to pray more, sleep less, curtail anger, and limit their words.[55] Throughout the sermon, the traits he praises are more associated with living a cenobitic, monastic life than an eremitic one. Such examples dominate the sermon, potentially revealing more about monastic life as lived in Bernard's day than they do any description of the actual hermit Saint Victor. In fact, neither sermon mentions concrete details about Victor's deeds or any miracles he may have

---

of St Victor," in Bernard of Clairvaux, *Treatises I*, CF 1:153–60, 165–67. However, it was not until Maître's publication of *Office de Saint Victor, Prologue à L'Antiphonaire, Lettre 398* in 2009 that they were placed in a more comprehensive framework including the "Office of Saint Victor." For discussion of the second Cistercian liturgical reform, see Maître, *Office de Saint Victor*, CF 527:49–66. All of the texts are included in that volume.

[54] SSV 1.1 (SBOp 6/1:30): *Sola est, cui gloria et iure debetur et secure impenditur.* Leclercq describes the various instances of word play in this text in "Introduction to *Sermones varii*," 153–54.

[55] SSV 1.3 (SBOp 6/1:31). In the translation below, the line reads, "Let us strive to bridle our anger, to limit our words, to sleep less, to pray more, [and] to *exhort one another with psalms, hymns, and spiritual songs*" (Col 3:16).

performed. Bernard instead emphasizes the spiritual message and the lessons learned from virtue.

One image that runs throughout the sermon is that of a banquet or feast that Victor provided with his life, one that nourishes and feeds those who come to the table. But, Bernard warns, one should not take what belongs to another: "I must not stretch out my hand to the glory of miracles, lest . . . I rightfully lose even what I seem to have received."[56] The lesson here is not to seize or take hold of those things that are beyond one's reach or strength. These things might overwhelm a person; therefore, one ought not to grasp for glory but should find what is truly set on the table. The psalms themselves here serve the meal: the bread of sorrow (Ps 126:2), the wine of compunction (Ps 59:5), and the bread of tears (Ps 41:4), "for I am poor and needy" (Ps 85:1).[57] Also served at the feast are the virtues of temperance, justice, prudence, and fortitude. These are served in honor of the host, Saint Victor, the one who invited everyone to the meal, but not all that is on offer is for everyone: "Take the drink and leave the gold," for just as the head of a household acts as an example to others, he also reserves the "privilege of miracles for himself."[58]

SECOND SERMON FOR THE FEAST OF SAINT VICTOR

While the first sermon focused on the imitation of Saint Victor's life, this sermon turns to his role in heaven, as the "merciful advocate" who can make intercession for humanity. Victor has turned from "motivator" (*incitator*) to "mediator" (*mediator*) and asks for nothing for himself but for the petitioner. During his earthly existence, he taught humanity how to live, and in heaven he is now the mediator

[56] SSV 1.4 (SBOp 6/1:31).

[57] SSV 1.5 (SBOp 6/1:32).

[58] SSV 1.5 (SBOp 6/1:32): *sume potum et pone aurum*. It goes on to say that the *Paterfamilias praerogativam sibi retineat in miraculis*. In addition to these virtues, the sermon includes a host of other monastic virtues, including chastity, silence, *ascetis*, and prayer, and Bernard also cites RB 7, on humility (see Leclercq, "Introduction to *Sermones varii*," 154).

who "invites us into glory."[59] The language in this sermon is both lyrical and precise, and Bernard integrated many passages into the "Office of Saint Victor."[60] The sermon contains many images of Victor in triumph; one that appears several times is that of a soldier who has retired, whose "sacred military service" has led to a magnificent crown. He dwells with the patriarch Abraham, and with Isaac and Jacob, in the kingdom of heaven. But this statement only explains where he is, whereas the manner of his heavenly existence has to do with his soul. Using texts from the Song of Songs, Bernard describes Victor's soul (*anima*): "she sits exalted and radiant, *filled with joy* . . . . she sits . . . *adorned with her jewels*. . . . She sits . . . free from cares, overflowing with delights."[61] The pronouns here are all feminine, since all of the descriptions describe the soul. This mystical language continues throughout the remainder of the paragraph and reflects the ethereal quality of the whole sermon.

Although Victor's struggle is over, he has not forgotten it, and he is still concerned for the living. His safety (in the heavenly kingdom) has not removed his compassion for those still in the fight. Having lived as a faithful disciple, following and serving Christ, now he has his reward, fellowship in the kingdom. But the difference between one who follows and the one who saves is clear: "the disciple does not contradict the teacher."[62] Saint Victor is not the teacher, but the disciple, and he did not achieve or merit anything on his own. Through his imitation of Christ he is both an example and a support to others as an advocate: "O Jesus the victor, we praise you in our Victor, knowing that it is you who won the victory in him!"[63] That is the focus

[59] SSV 2.1 (SBOp 6/1:33): *Factus est mediator ad regnum, qui fuit incitator ad opus.*

[60] The sources of the text for the Office are mapped out in a convenient chart in Maître, *Office de Saint Victor*, SCh 527:81–82. Also see Leclercq, "Saint Bernard Écrivain," 163–64. He includes an excellent discussion of Bernard's language in this sermon.

[61] SSV 2.2 (SBOp 6/1:34).

[62] SSV 2.3 (SBOp 6/1:35): *Non est discipulus contra Magistrum.*

[63] SSV 2.5 (SBOp 6/1:36). This sermon is not the place for a theological discussion on the relationship between Christ and the saints, but Bernard discusses the matter elsewhere. Raciti points out that the difference between them is found clearly in his statement that a human being can communicate the good but is not its ultimate teacher, a point he also makes in *On Grace and Free Choice*, 1 (SBOp 3:166). See Raciti's discussion in *Sermons variés*, SCh 526:124.

for Bernard always, the imitation of Christ, exemplified in the example of the saints, inspiring sinners.

Sermon Six: On the Will of God

Context

"On the Will of God" was one of the six sermons from this collection that Mabillon published in the seventeenth century, placing it among Bernard's liturgical sermons and designating it as the sixth sermon in Lent.[64] Since Bernard himself did not include this text in the final redaction of this major liturgical collection, it does not belong to that series. Therefore, the SBOp editors moved it and placed it among the *Sermones varii* (SBOp 6/1:37–39). It does, however, contain many themes present in the Lenten sermons for the liturgical year. Motifs such as overcoming obstacles, devotion to prayer, and an emphasis on learning appear prominently in this sermon; it might therefore be considered a short meditation on Lent.[65]

Content

The focal point of this sermon is the biblical passage "your will be done," and therefore this text could be considered a meditation on the Lord's Prayer (Matt 6:10). The theme Bernard pursues throughout is unification of the human will with the will of God (*voluntas Domini*). While the angels have already achieved this union with divine will, he says, human "consummation" must overcome many obstacles in order to realize a similar unification. Of the many obstacles that stand in the way, all share a common problem, with the same root cause, the

[64] PL 183:824D. See also Raciti's comments in his introduction to this sermon, *Sermons variés*, SCh 526:205.

[65] For a discussion of Bernard's liturgical sermons for Lent, see Wim Verbaal's introduction to Bernard, *Sermons for Lent and the Easter Season*, CF 52:xii–xxix. Verbaal notes that in the final version of Bernard's Lenten sermons the theme of fighting against weakness, ignorance, and the overestimation of the self indicates that "Lent may thus be considered a battle," xxix.

fundamental disorder of the passions. The Augustinian concept of "disordered love" lies at the heart of the divergence between human and divine will, Bernard says, and he identifies the four major barriers that result from that disorder: malice, weakness, avarice, and ignorance (SBOp 6/1:37–39).[66] The way to address each impediment, he explains, is to apply corrective and restorative action exemplified by the four cardinal virtues: justice, fortitude, temperance, and prudence.

The message of this sermon is one of encouragement and hope, as Bernard calls his monks to embrace virtue as a way to bring about the injunction of the Lord's Prayer, "your will be done." But since the human will has become "crooked and convoluted" and gained an inclination toward evil, he says, it is no longer compatible with the "perfectly upright" (*rectissima*) will of God (SBOp 6/1:38). Malice divides humanity from God and also causes division among people. This vice leads to envy, enmity, dissension, and even taking satisfaction in being mean to others. Since the human will contains an "evil inclination and lust for doing harm," it must be corrected by justice, so that it can cut off "poisonous growths with a pruning hook" (SBOp 6/1:38). This is an ongoing, constant battle, and although it is impossible completely to eradicate these growths in this life, justice serves as a corrective and instructive virtue.

Bodily weakness is also a barrier to unifying human will with God's, since physical pain can cause human will to be "at odds with God's will." The remedy is fortitude, which curtails resistance to divine will and strengthens human resolve. Other impediments associated with errant desires, such as avarice (*concupiscentia*), spring from a fundamentally disordered love.[67] The deformed will becomes "crooked and

[66] The Latin terms are *malitia, infirmitas, concupiscentia,* and *ignorantia*; they can be contrasted with the opposite virtues, *iustitia, fortitudo, temperantia,* and *prudentia.*

[67] The English translation for the Latin term *concupiscentia* in this volume is *appetite.* While that is an acceptable translation, the Latin term carries with it a more negative aspect associated with the idea of carnal desire or a lust for things of the world. Therefore, it can also be translated with the English words *lust, avarice,* or even *covetousness.* The French translation uses the term *la convoitise,* which means covetousness or greed; see *Sermons variés,* SCh 526:209. In the German version, Gerhard Winkler translates the term as *die Begierde,* which also carries with it a negative sense and implies an aspect of sexual immorality akin to lust (*Bernhard von Clairvaux:*

convoluted," in such a way that it causes one to focus on the earthly rather than the divine. Whether one wills something good or bad, the impetus to do either begins with a fallen will, ruled by an errant desire associated with avarice and lust. Temperance can combat this inclination in the will by helping to constrain it, tempering disordered desire and tamping down lust.

The final obstacle to the unification of human and divine will is ignorance. Here ignorance refers to lack of knowledge concerning God's will. The corrective virtue, Bernard explains, is prudence, which makes divine will known little by little and is thus progressive, allowing one to grow in the knowledge of God's will. This will result in knowing what is acceptable to God (SBOp 6/1:39).

The restoration of the human will requires the intervention of divine grace, but it also needs the consent of human free choice. When the two cooperate, one can live a life of grace, in which the exercise of virtue helps to combat disorder within the will introduced by sin. The ultimate goal, therefore, is for humanity to possess what the angels already have, one will, unified with God: "the consummation of the virtues will consummate a union so happy and so desirable that between us and God there will be but one will, and whatever pleases him will also please us."[68] The process of conforming human will to God's begins in this life but must wait for its final unification in the next.

The action and necessity of grace is primary with respect to restoring the will, but this sermon does not directly express this idea, leaving it implicit in discussing the exercise of virtue. Bernard had developed this theme in his earlier treatise *On Grace and Free Choice*, where he emphasized the necessity of grace in order to gain "freedom from sin," which he also calls "freedom of counsel."[69] Although the will, he says,

---

Sämtliche Werke, 9:127). I have chosen to use the word *avarice* here, especially since this sermon is discussing the opposing categories of vice and virtue.

[68] SBOp 6/1:39: *Sic virtutum consummatione, unionem illam tam felicem, tam desiderabilem consummabit, ut sit nobis cum Deo una voluntas, et quaecumque et placent, placeant simul et nobis.*

[69] *Liberum arbitrium*, free choice, is a key concept in *On Grace and Free Choice* (Gra 16; cf. Gra 4.10).

is "captive to sin," which makes it impossible to choose the good, free choice (*liberum arbitrium*) is still part of the natural state of humanity, which Bernard calls a "self-determining habit of the soul."[70] Therefore, freedom of choice was not lost in the Fall, nor will it be relinquished in heaven, but it is weighed down in this life as a result of original sin. Even in its fallen state, however, the will can still give voluntary consent to grace, because it remains free (Gra 12).

In this sermon the "destruction of human nature" refers to the aspect of the image of God lost in the Fall. These include the "freedom from sin" and the "freedom from sorrow" (Gra 3). Freedom from sin can be restored at least partially in this life by free choice's consenting to work with grace in the exercise of virtue, allowing the human will to move closer to God's will.

Sermon Seven: On the Mercies of the Lord

Context

Like the previous sermon, "On the Mercies of the Lord" was one of the six sermons in this collection published by Mabillon. He placed it among Bernard's liturgical sermons, where it appeared as the second sermon for the sixth Sunday after Pentecost.[71] When Leclercq published his updated Latin critical edition, he moved this sermon to the *Sermons varii*. This sermon reads more like a sermon from the *De diversis* collection than a monastic sermon for the liturgical year, but the content is unmistakably Bernard's.

[70] Gra 2.3. See Bernard McGinn's Introduction to *On Grace and Free Choice*, CF 3 (Kalamazoo, MI: Cistercian Publications, 1977), 26–32. McGinn provides a good explanation of Bernard's concept of Adam's sin in relation to Augustine, followed by an overview of Bernard's concept of the human being after the Fall.

[71] Leclercq points out that this sermon appears in some manuscript witnesses to the Pf collection, where it contains a different and briefer treatment of the seven mercies of God. See SBOp 6/1:5, and also see Raciti's remarks in his introduction to this sermon, *Sermons Variés*, SCh 526:219.

Content

Addressing his monks, Bernard warns, "ingratitude is a deadly thing," since it is an enemy of grace and salvation; it is particularly repulsive to God when harbored by those who are "children of grace" and "people of conversion" (those in the monastic community).[72] Therefore, one ought to be grateful for God's mercies and act in a manner that befits a posture of thankfulness. Such behavior means avoiding the extremes of levity or excessive laughter, as well as undoing sorrow or unhappiness. The mercies of God, Bernard explains, are "gifts of grace"; they help to combat evil, but ingratitude blocks grace so that it can no longer find a pathway into the heart.

The first of the mercies of God discussed in this sermon is the gift of protection from sin. After humanity had fallen into sin, God in his love and kindness fortified them against further sin, so that, Bernard says, even when he was rebellious, God "upheld me by his grace . . . he protected me from additional sins, defiant and disdainful though I was."[73] The second mercy is that God turns away or "pretends not to notice" human sin.[74] Bernard does not develop this idea further here, but in a sermon for the liturgical year called "Fragments [which are] the Seven Mercies," he fleshes the image out to a greater degree. In that sermon he also explains that the second of God's mercies involves delaying his vengeance and pondering forgiveness of human sin.[75]

[72] SBOp 6/1:40: *Peremptoria siquidem res est ingratitudo; filiis gratiae, in hominibus conversionis.*

[73] SBOp 6/1:42: *sic gratia conservabat, quod in multis contrarium et contemnentem nihilominus ab aliis benignissime protegebat?* Posed as a question here, *ab aliis* means "from others" and refers to *peccatum*, meaning "sin," which appears earlier in the text, so "from additional sins."

[74] The Latin *dissimulo* is a verb meaning "to conceal or hide or keep secret." The English translation here is excellent, well capturing the meaning that God "pretends not to notice" human sin.

[75] SBOp 6/1:210; see also Beverley Kienzle's translation of the sermon in Bernard of Clairvaux's *Sermons for the Summer Season*, CF 53 (Kalamazoo, MI: Cistercian Publications, 1991), 123. In this sermon, the mercies of God are expressed as loaves of bread.

The third mercy Bernard presents is a change of heart in the recipient, so that what was previously considered good or sweet (*dulcis*) is now bad or bitter, and this transformation leads one to repentance. Repentance on its own is not sufficient, however, and it is ineffective unless it is accompanied by God's fourth mercy, which is forgiveness and remittance of sin. The fifth mercy, also a gift of grace, is the gift of strength to encourage self-restraint; this gift is God's power to remove the "yoke of sin" from the necks of sinners. The strength provided by this mercy is not human agency or action but the power of God, who has given five graces to combat sin and evil. As the monks progress in their spiritual lives, they fight against sin in order to progress on their journey to grow closer to God. Grace supports them on their journey, and they must be grateful for all of God's mercies.

Bernard discusses the final two of the seven mercies briefly at the end of the sermon; both are a kind of culmination of the others. The "grace to acquire merits" is the sixth. It is the overall goal of the initial five, which are given to help the recipient, to allow a change to living a good life (*bonae conversationis*). Here Bernard alludes to the monastic ideal of *conversatio morum*, a commitment to living a conversion of life, an ongoing commitment to reforming one's life in order to attain the goal of living a good life.[76] Such attainment is not possible without divine grace, and therefore the sermon contains no hint of Pelagianism. The final of the seven divine mercies is hope, an eschatological aspiration that allows even a sinner a glimpse of God's goodness and allows for the hope of heaven.

Sermon Eight: On the Seven Gifts of the Holy Spirit

Context

As this sermon focuses on a spiritual theme, it is not associated with a specific season of the liturgical year. Of all the sermons in this collection it is by far the longest; its rich imagery and elaborate allegory

[76] RB 58.17: *Suscipiendus autem in oratorio coram omnibus promittat de stabilitate sua et conversatione morum suorum et oboedientia.* "Let the one being received promise before all in the oratory stability, conversion of life, and obedience."

read like a story. It reflects Bernard's oral or preaching style rather than the beautiful prose characteristic of his literary sermons.[77] Some scholars consider it a summary, with ideas borrowed from chapters 10 and 11 of *On the Nature and Dignity of Love*, a work written by Bernard's friend, William of Saint-Thierry (d. 1148).[78] Although they contain several closely related passages that demonstrate parallel ideas, it is not clear whether Bernard's or William's was written first.[79] It is possible that this sermon was written by a secretary rather than by Bernard.[80]

This is another of the sermons that did not appear in Mabillon's edition. As a result, it remained unpublished until it was included in SBOp's *Sermones varii*.[81] Leclercq established the manuscript tradition in SBOp and demonstrated that the sermon was preserved in two manuscript families associated with the series M, the second recension of Bernard's liturgical sermons.[82] This external evidence, taken in conjunction with the internal evidence, including the connection with William's treatise, has led to general acceptance of the sermon as Bernard's (SBOp 6/1:6).

[77] Raciti, *Sermons variés*, SCh 526:233. For Bernard's oral preaching style, see Jean Leclercq, "Introduction to Bernard's Sermons *De diversis*," trans. Elias Dietz, CSQ 42, no. 1 (2007): 37–62, esp. 38–39. See also Holdsworth, "Were the Sermons," 295–318.

[78] Henri Rochais, "Énquête sur les Sermons divers et les Sentences de S. Bernard," *Analecta Cisterciensis* 18 (1962): 120–30. This article includes a close reading of the sermon and compares its ideas to William's text (126–29). Heinrich Weisweiler had tried to make the argument that this sermon was merely a summary of William's, but Rochais disproved this position (126). The connection between the two works is also cited by Jean Leclercq, "Introduction to *Sermones varii*," CSQ 43:158.

[79] What is clear is that there were many shared ideas; see Rochais, "Enquête sur les Sermons divers," 126. This connection helps to establish the sermon's authenticity.

[80] Leclercq argues this point in "Introduction to *Sermones varii*," 158. Translators have noted some of the issues in the Latin text.

[81] In addition to this sermon, the other sermons Mabillon omitted are "For Advent" and "For Epiphany." Both of these as well as this one were included in the *Sermones varii* in SBOp 6/1. The other sermon in this collection, "In natali Sancti Benedicti," was published by Gaetano Raciti in 1998 and does not appear in the SBOp edition.

[82] SBOp 6/1:6. Leclercq determined that this sermon was included in many "old witnesses" of the series M (Media), associated with the "zone of Morimond," where many of the oldest manuscripts are found.

Scholarly reactions to this sermon are mixed; some scholars consider it a good example of Bernard's exceptional pedagogy, with Leclercq calling it a "simple and clear parable," while Raciti views it as "not the best of Saint Bernard."[83] What can be said is that the text is neither simple nor straightforward, and the analogies are lengthy and involved. It seems as though it would take a good deal of concentration to follow the development of the images and remain focused on their meaning while listening to the sermon. Nonetheless, the ideas are clearly Bernard's.

Content

From the opening line of this sermon Bernard's focus is clear: "The Mediator between God and humanity, Jesus Christ . . . chose to use the seven gifts of the Holy Spirit to reconcile the human race."[84] Reconciling humankind to God and making satisfaction for the disobedience of Adam, Bernard explains, is the role of the Mediator, and the seven gifts of the Holy Spirit are given to humanity to help heal the rupture between the two parties. The central and overarching question of this sermon is, "why did God become human?" The classic formulation and answer to this question was offered in the eleventh century by Anselm of Canterbury in *Why God Became Man (Cur Deus Homo?)*. While Bernard never quotes directly from this work here, the argumentative parallels are unmistakable.

[83] Raciti: "il appartient à sa prédication orale et n'est pas, pensons-nous, 'du meilleur Saint Bernard'" (SCh 526:233). Leclercq writes that Bernard "explained . . . through a simple and clear parable that does credit to the author's sense of pedagogy" ("Introduction to *Sermones varii*," 159).

[84] SBOp 6/1:44: *Mediator Dei et hominum, homo Christus Iesus, qua convenientia et necessitate, in reconciliatione humani generis, septem Sancti Spiritus donis uti voluerit.* The seven gifts of the Holy Spirit figure prominently in some of Bernard's other sermons; see for example Sermon 2 for the Annunciation 2 (Ann 2) (SBOp 4:348–49); Sermon 3 for Easter (Pasc 3) (SBOp 5:109). For the seven gifts of the Holy Spirit as a corrective to faults, see S 14 (Div 14) in the *Monastic Sermons* (*De diversis*), SBOp 6/1:134–39.

The sermon's structure follows Isaiah 11:2, with the Isaian themes taken up in reverse order, beginning with the fear of the Lord and ending with the spirit of wisdom: "The spirit of the Lord shall rest on him, the spirit of wisdom and understanding, the spirit of counsel and might, the spirit of knowledge [and of piety] and the fear of the Lord."[85] Beginning with the spirit of fear, Bernard takes each of the first five gifts—fear, piety, knowledge, counsel, and might—and explains them in the context of the role of Christ as the Mediator between God and humankind. As the Mediator, he positioned himself to represent the interests of both parties. On the one hand, he was subordinate to God, subject to him by the spirit of fear (*spiritum timoris*), in order to show "faithful reverence" to the Father. On the other hand, Christ descended to join humanity in order to show "merciful compassion" (*spiritum pietatis misericordi*).[86] In this way he had a connection to both humanity and God and was a partner to each side in the dispute. The tie, however, was greater with God, with whom Christ shared the bond of fear and of love (*timore et amore*), resulting in a double connection with one side. Therefore, the two sides were not equal but reflected a dispute similar to that between a lord and a servant (SBOp 6/1:44).

In order to determine what he owed to each, the Mediator had to rely on what Bernard calls the "whole spirit of knowledge" (*spiritus scientiae*), the same knowledge that Adam had possessed but rejected.[87] Connected to both humanity and God, the Mediator had to navigate sometimes competing priorities held in a dynamic tension. Discerning God's will and prioritizing it required him to use his knowledge

[85] The quotation is taken from the New Revised Standard Version of the Bible, but the English text does not include the term *pietas* in verse two. The Latin Vulgate retains this term, as it follows the Greek Septuagint text, which includes the word εὐσεβείας, translated into Latin as *pietas* and English *piety*. Also, for the phrase *spirit of fear*, one must read beyond verse two in the Vulgate: *et requiescet super eum spiritus Domini spiritus* ***sapientiae*** *et* ***intellectus*** *spiritus* ***consilii*** *et* ***fortitudinis*** *spiritus* ***scientiae*** *et* ***pietatis*** [vv. 2–3] *et replebit eum spiritus* ***timoris*** *Domini*. For a discussion of the "spirit of counsel," see John R. Sommerfeldt, *Bernard of Clairvaux: On the Life of the Mind* (New York/Mahwah, NJ: Newman Press), 59–68.

[86] For the English translation of *pietas*, see the translator's note below.

[87] SBOp 6/1:44–45: *totum spiritum scientiae procuratum est.*

(*scientia*) and to act accordingly to defeat the devil and save humanity. This action was the opposite of what Adam had done in choosing a "disordered devotion," disobeying God and casting humanity into bondage and captivity. The Mediator, Bernard says, needs strength, the gift of fortitude to liberate the captive (*captivum liberandum fortitudine*) and defeat the strong man, the devil.[88]

Bernard's discussion of the spirit of counsel (*spiritus consilii*) engages the central theme of the sermon and of book 2 of Anselm's treatise: "how can humanity pay the debt incurred by Adam?"[89]

Bernard's Argument

- Since the sin of humanity was so great, no sacrifice could "appease God on its own." Only one equal to God could pay the debt for humanity, and Christ was equal to God (Phil 2:6; John 10:30).
- In order to pay this debt, the Mediator also "needed to have something to offer" that was not from his divinity but from humanity. He took on human nature in order to make a sacrifice that would "abolish the sentence" and reconcile humanity to God (Col 2:14). However, his human nature had to be "pure from every stain of sin." By the "spirit of counsel," a new type of combat was established: dying destroyed death, the devil was condemned, and humanity was reconciled to God through the voluntary death of the Mediator.
- The Mediator was uniquely qualified to take on this role because he was divine and coequal with God. By his voluntary sacrifice of himself and by his acceptance of his human nature as the "first-born brother" (Rom 8:29), he purchased "another by the price of his sacrifice," out of his love for humanity.

[88] SBOp 6/1:45. The devil is both strong (*fortis*) and well-armed (*armatus*).

[89] *Cur Deus Homo*, in *Opera Omnia*, ed. F. S. Schmitt, vol. II (Edinburgh: T. Nelson, 1946). See in English, *Anselm of Canterbury: The Major Works*, ed. Brian Davies and G. R. Evans (Oxford: Oxford University Press, 1998). All citations appear with the standard abbreviation, CDH (*Cur Deus Homo*), followed by the book and chapter numbers. This reference will allow access to most versions of Anselm's text.

Anselm's argument

- Adam's sin violated God's honor; as a result, all of humanity incurred a debt that had to be paid. Humanity must make recompense because they were the ones who had incurred the debt. In God's abundant mercy, he could have simply forgiven the debt, but this action would have violated justice. In order to preserve both mercy and justice, punishment and payment were required, but accompanied by divine forgiveness.[90]
- In their fallen state, humanity cannot pay the debt they owe, as only one without sin can pay the debt on behalf of humanity. Only God or one equal to God can make satisfaction and restore humanity.[91]
- The God-man is necessary and uniquely qualified to pay the debt on behalf of humanity.[92] Therefore, he gives himself voluntarily to make satisfaction for the debt (sin) of humanity, and in so doing, he redeems humankind.[93] God's honor is restored and justice preserved, because sin is punished and the debt is paid.

The guiding principle of Anselm's text is a long rational argument about the Fall and redemption of humanity through a dialogue with his counterpart. Bernard's goal, however, is much different. He presents ideas to instruct and teach rather than to expound a reasoned argument. His language is biblical, and he bases all his proofs on passages from Scripture. Although the contexts and motivations of the two works differ, Anselm's language conceptualizing human debt and God's justice, as well as the idea of making "satisfaction" for sin, are all apparent in Bernard's sermon. The problem with attempting to identify the source of Bernard's argument is that he almost never acknowledges his sources.[94]

[90] Anselm, CDH I.24; II:20.

[91] Anselm, CDH II.6.

[92] Anselm, CDH II.4.

[93] Anselm, CDH II.11.

[94] Anthony N. S. Lane, *Bernard of Clairvaux: Theologian of the Cross*, CS 248 (Collegeville, MN: Cistercian Publications, 2013), 191. See esp. Lane's description of "The

Having discussed the first five gifts of the spirit, Bernard introduces the final two, understanding and wisdom, through a lengthy allegorical illustration that represents God's plan for the redemption and salvation of humanity. Imagine, Bernard says, a person whose body is withering away but whose head retains its health. The senses located in the head, sight, hearing, and smell, are fully functional and healthy, while the body deteriorates in sickness. The sense of taste is also lost, and its lack leaves the body unable to benefit from food, regardless of how much is eaten. If, however, the senses of the head move down into taste, reviving it, the appetite can rebound, and food can once again be efficacious, restoring the body to health. This is analogous to the human situation, with the head representing the soul and the body the state of humanity, sick with sin. The health of the soul represents the way in which God remained active in creation after the Fall of humanity.

In order to complete the image of healing, Bernard connects human attributes with God's plan for salvation: "the eyes symbolize angels," which represents their ability to illuminate, the patriarchs are the ears, which listened to God, and the prophets are the nostrils, which breathed in divine inspiration and told of the coming of Christ. The wisdom of God corresponds with taste, and the flavor hidden in the taste is Christ. Christ is the Mediator who pours out the "dew of spiritual graces" on the church, which is the body (Eph 1:22-23). These graces invigorate the whole with love so that "daily progress towards salvation" can be made until the whole body of the church attains perfect health and arrives at perfect humanity in the fullness of Christ.[95]

Cross as Satisfaction for Our Sins," 190–96. Cf. Gillian Evans, *The Life of the Mind: St. Bernard of Clairvaux* (Oxford: Oxford University Press, 1983), 156–59.

[95] SBOp 6/1:49. *Nunc autem, ipso mediatore, spiritualium rore gratiam ubertim ecclesiam, . . . desideria eius per caritatem inflammante, in salutem quotidie proficit, donec, vere perfecta totius corporis sanitate, omnes occurramus in virum perfectum, in mensura aetatis plenitudinis Christi* (Eph 4:13). Wim Verbaal has placed Bernard's epistolary corpus in the context of other twelfth-century letter collections; he argues that Bernard's collection reflects a conscious intentionality and portrays a man "attempting to bring order into the world . . . within the spiritual core that is the monastery." These letter collections, therefore, represent more than a chronological record or a narrative of events; they reveal the qualities of the compiler(s) and the "messages and what they wanted to

Sermon Nine: On Saint Malachy

Context

Bishop Malachy of Armagh (d. 1148) was a monk, bishop, reformer, and close friend of Bernard of Clairvaux. Several texts in Bernard's writings attest to Bernard's respect and fondness for Malachy. The most famous of these is the *Vita*, the *Life of Saint Malachy* (MalV), written after Malachy's death at Clairvaux on November 2, 1148.[96]

Because Malachy died in November, this sermon appeared at the end of the liturgical year and is therefore placed last among the *Sermones varii* in SBOp. This sermon is here placed in the penultimate position because the newly authenticated, "For the Feast of Saint Benedict," appears as the final sermon in this book.

In addition to the *Vita*, Bernard wrote two sermons, a hymn, an epitaph, and several letters to Malachy.[97] Of the two sermons in his honor, only the first, composed on the occasion of Malachy's death, appears among Bernard's liturgical sermons.[98] Because this second sermon for Malachy was not among the edited collection of Bernard's sermons, SBOp included it in *Sermones varii*. Bernard composed the sermon for the one-year anniversary of Malachy's death. Scholars

---

convey" ("Voicing your Voice: The Fiction of a Life. Early Twelfth-Century Letter Collections and the Case of Bernard of Clairvaux," *Interfaces* 4 [2017]: 103–24, here 121, 103).

[96] *Vita Sancti Malachiae*, SBOp 3:297–378. For the English translation, see Bernard of Clairvaux, *The Life and Death of Saint Malachy the Irishman*, trans. Robert T. Meyer, CF 10 (Kalamazoo, MI: Cistercian Publications, 1978). On Bernard's relationship with Malachy, see Brian Patrick McGuire, *The Difficult Saint: Bernard of Clairvaux & His Tradition*, chap. 3, "Bernard and Malachy Reconsidered, Intimacy or Confraternity?" CS 126 (Kalamazoo, MI: Cistercian Publications, 1991), 75–106.

[97] SBOp 5:417, n. 5, lists Bernard's works on Malachy, all of which begin with the first three letters of his name, "Mal," followed by a letter or Roman numeral designating the specific work. The "Hymn for Malachy's Feast" is MalH, and the "Epitaph" is MalE; the other sermon, written on the occasion of Malachy's funeral, is MAlT, and this sermon is MalS. For the letters concerning Malachy, see especially Bernard's letter sent to Ireland on the occasion of Malachy's death, Ep 374; see also Epp 341, 356, 357, and 545. All appear in SBOp 8.

[98] SBOp 5:417–23.

accept its authenticity, and its manuscript transmission is well established.[99] Finally, in addition to the two sermons written for the Feast of Saint Victor, this is the only other sermon in the collection for which we have a clear date. Malachy died in 1148; this sermon was written after his death.

Content

Although this sermon commemorates the death of Saint Malachy, its tone is one of joy and praise rather than sorrow. Bernard explains that Malachy had achieved a good deal in his life; not only was he an active reformer of the church in Ireland, but he also faithfully executed his duties as bishop, never forgetting the poor or weak and maintaining an active prayer life of introspection and recollection. As a reformer, Malachy re-introduced the sacraments of penance, confirmation, and marriage, and he challenged ecclesiastical corruption, such as hereditary abbacies and lax liturgical practices.[100] During his trip to Rome in 1140, seeking the pallium for both Cashel and Armagh, he was appointed papal legate by Pope Innocent II.[101] On his way home, Malachy stopped at Clairvaux; here he met Bernard and became enamored with Cistercian monastic life. Although he desired to remain at Clairvaux and join the community, Innocent denied his request. He left some of his companions at Clairvaux, however; they eventually returned to Ireland and founded Mellifont Abbey. Malachy's dream

[99] SBOp 6/1:6. Also see Callerot, *Sermons variés*, SCh 526:260.

[100] See the Introduction to *The Life and Death of Saint Malachy*, CF 10:4.

[101] The *pallium* is a circular ecclesiastical vestment, worn by metropolitan bishops as a symbol of their status and position. The pallium itself is worn over the shoulders: "it is a band of white that encircled the shoulders and fell in two strips on the chest and back" (Steven A. Schoenig, *Bonds of Wool: The Pallium and Papal Power in the Middle Ages* [Washington, DC: The Catholic University of America Press, 2017], 3). See also Maureen Miller, *Clothing the Clergy: Virtue and Power in Medieval Europe c. 800–1200* (Ithaca, NY: Cornell University Press, 2014). The pallia were finally bestowed on the bishops of Armagh and Cashel at the Council of Kells in 1152, four years after Malachy's death.

to remain at Clairvaux was finally realized when, on another trip to Rome, he stopped once again at Clairvaux, dying there in 1148. Bernard preached his funeral Mass and composed this sermon in memory of his friend, one year after his death.

The connection between Bernard and Malachy was one of mutual respect and admiration, as is clearly evidenced in this sermon. In many ways, Bernard saw Malachy as both a model of ecclesiastical service and one deeply rooted in prayer, faithful to his inner spiritual life. The interplay between the words *minister* (*minister*) and *ministry* (*ministerium*) emerges in the first part of the text, where Bernard describes Malachy as a "faithful minister," with a "fruitful ministry."[102] He explained that Christ as Savior received from Malachy a ministry offered freely, and the Savior was "pleased with the ministry's success at converting sinners.[103]

In what may be the best line of the sermon, Bernard praises Malachy's virtues, in particular, the mercy he showed to the poor: "He was poor with himself but rich to the poor."[104] Malachy's attitude toward giving was likewise cheerful, and he acted as a peacemaker, settling disputes between people, meting out compassion and correction as the case necessitated. But he was not afraid to take on tyrants, and he acted as a teacher to kings or princes when necessary. Just as zealously as he confronted the powerful, he was also a "hen warming and protecting her chicks" (Matt 23:37). He gathered all and did not discriminate, looking after all regardless of age, sex, or social rank.

[102] This play on words is discussed in most introductions to this text; see e.g. Callerot's comments on "The Meditations" in the text of *Sermons variés*, SCh 526:255. Also see Leclercq, "Introduction to Bernard's *Sermones varii*," 160. In Bernard's *Five Books On Consideration, Advice to a Pope* (Csi), he also uses a similar kind of play on the words associated with ministry, such as the verb *ministrare* and the noun, *ministerium*. For example, in Csi 2.11, Bernard contrasts terms associated with rulership, *dominare* and *dominium*, to remind the pope of his ministry. See SBOp 3:418 and additional discussion below.

[103] SBOp 6/1:51: *Ergo in ministro quidem gratum munus gratuitum, in ministerio autem placita conversio peccatorum.*

[104] SBOp 6/1:51: *Pauper sibi, sed dives pauperibus erat.*

Bernard praises Malachy's ministry, but one of the essential qualities he identifies as most necessary for good ecclesiastical leadership is self-knowledge. This is the same point he made to Pope Eugenius III in his five letters, now identified as books, in *Five Books On Consideration: Advice to a Pope*. Bernard wrote to Eugenius in the same period (1145–1153) as he was writing on Malachy, and he urged him to know himself and to consider who he was before beginning his ministry.[105] The sermon on Malachy contains some of the same themes; of Malachy Bernard observes, "He was his own master," in effect meaning that he acted with intent rather than compulsion, he controlled his temper, and he exercised discipline and caution. Self-knowledge also helped Malachy when he protected himself so that he could belong both to himself and to others.[106] Bernard encouraged this same quality in the pope: "since everyone possesses you, make sure that you too are among the possessors" (Csi 1.6; SBOp 3:399).

When Malachy had free time, Bernard says, he did not take a holiday from meditation, fervent prayer, or even "the leisure of contemplation." During his leisure time, he still maintained his modest demeanor and was not given to frivolousness; his speech was serious and his smile restrained. Ensuring time for contemplation is essential to good ministry, and although Bernard does not develop this idea further here, he makes its importance clear in his advice to Eugenius.[107] Malachy's feast honors his many virtues, and even after his death, Bernard says, he acts as an advocate: "the heavenly court now contains one of our own." His light shines in the darkness through his miracles and merits.

[105] Bernard declared that self-knowledge was important for the pope, *De consideratione*, 1.6–7; 2.5–7 (SBOp 3:401, 414). For the English, see Bernard of Clairvaux, *Five Books on Consideration: Advice to a Pope*, trans. John Anderson and Elizabeth Kennan, CF 37 (Kalamazoo, MI: Cistercian Publications), 32–33, 36. Pope Eugenius III had been Bernard's novice, then beginning in 1140 abbot of the Cistercian house at Tre Fontane, outside of Rome. When he was elected pope in 1145, Bernard wrote him the series of letters instructing him in his duties, now known as *De consideratione*. For a discussion of Bernard, self-knowledge, and humility, see John R. Sommerfeldt, *Bernard of Clairvaux: On the Life of the Mind*, 92–97, 102–3.

[106] SBOp 6/1:52. As his "own master," *Erat suimet potis*; "As one who guarded himself," *Seipsum custodiebat*.

[107] Csi 2.5; 1.12 (SBOp 3:414, 407).

Sermon Ten: For the Feast of Saint Benedict

Context

Is it possible that Bernard wrote only one sermon for the Feast of Saint Benedict? Until recently, the answer has been yes. Bernard's only previously known sermon for this important feast appears at the very beginning of the fifth volume of the SBOp.[108] In 1998, Gaetano Raciti published an article about a "new sermon" written for the Feast of Saint Benedict, called "Verba lectionis huius" (VLH).[109] In his article, Raciti established a convincing case for attributing authorship of the VLH to Bernard. On the basis of his work, this sermon was included in the French collection of the *Sermons variés* published in Sources Chrétiennes in 2010.[110] The sermon was well known to scholars such as Jean Leclercq, the great Bernadine specialist and co-editor of SBOp, but he rejected the sermon as inauthentic.[111] As he had established his objections almost a decade before compiling volume 6 of SBOp, the sermon does not appear in the *Sermones varii* collection.

Raciti began his investigation with an examination of the manuscript evidence, evaluating sixteen manuscripts containing the VLH,

[108] SBOp 5:1–12. See Verbaal's comments in the introduction to Bernard's *Sermons for Lent and the Easter Season*, CF 52:xiv–xv.

[109] Raciti, "Un nouveau sermon." The sermon takes its name from its first three words, following Peter's words from Matthew 19:27: "Look, we have left everything and followed you."

[110] Bernard de Clairvaux, *Sermons variés*, SCh 526. In the French version, the sermon appears according to its chronological place in the liturgy, after the second of the two sermons "Pour La Fête de Saint Victor," celebrated February 26, and "Pour la fête de saint Benoît," March 21. This sermon does not appear in the German or Italian translations.

[111] See Raciti's discussion, "Un nouveau sermon," 64. Cf. Jean Leclercq, "Les collections de sermons de Nicholas de Clairvaux," *Recueil d'études*, 1:52–54, 60. Raciti discovered this new sermon some years before he published the article in 1993, when he came across a page attributed to Bernard while collating manuscript variants in the sermons of Aelred of Rievaulx. This initial discovery led to a long-term project to uncover and authenticate the sermon as an authentic work of Bernard. The culmination of that work was the 1998 article. He includes the brief account of discovery in "Un nouveau sermon," 61, n. 5. Jean Leclercq died in 1993, before Raciti published his findings.

which he divided into four families. He discovered that many of these manuscripts attributed the sermon to Bernard, and that where there was no direct reference to him, the sermon was nonetheless not credited to anyone else. Furthermore, he supplemented this external evidence with internal textual arguments that demonstrated that the sermon contains interpretations of scriptural themes similar to Bernard's in other works, as well as doctrinal and literary similarities to those other works.[112] In addition, Raciti showed that the VLH was a common source for two sermons, each written by monks at Clairvaux, both of whom were secretaries of Bernard: Geoffrey of Auxerre (d. ca. 1188) and Nicholas of Clairvaux (i.e., Nicolas of Montiéramey) (d. 1176/1178).[113] In two detailed appendices, Raciti highlights the textual parallels between each of the works and VLH.[114] This sermon is the final work in this English translation of the *Various Sermons*, titled "For the Feast of Saint Benedict" (BenV).

An earlier English translation of the VLH appeared in 2001, with a summary of Raciti's 1998 article and a brief overview of the sermon, followed by the English text.[115] The 2001 English version is not the same as the translation in this volume, but it offers some additional insights, including biblical references that complement Raciti's 1998 version. The paragraph numbering for the 2001 version also differs, as it is based on the VLH Latin text from 1998. In the current volume, "For the Feast of Saint Benedict" and its paragraph numbering follow the 2010 French version in Sources Chrétiennes, *Sermons variés.*

[112] Raciti, "Un nouveau sermon," 67. From the sixteen manuscripts, Raciti identified an "archetype" for each of the four families of manuscripts (68–71). This was the basis for his Latin text.

[113] For a more complete analysis and comparison of the sermons and letters of Bernard and Nicholas of Montiéramey, see the extensive discussion and meticulously compiled appendices in De Gussem, "Bernard of Clairvaux and Nicholas of Montiéramey," S210–S25.

[114] Raciti, "Un nouveau sermon," 106–7. In the appendices on these two pages, Raciti compares both Geoffrey of Auxerre's text, *De colloquio Symonis de Iesu*, and Nicolas's, *In huius Patris nostri*, with the VLH. Geoffrey's is found in *Entretien de Simon-Pierre avec Jésus*, Intro. and annot. Henri Rochais, SCh 364 (Paris: Les Éditions du Cerf, 1990). For Nicolas's text, see *In huius Patris nostri*, PL 144:548C–53B.

[115] Francis R. Swietek and John R. Sommerfeldt, "A 'New' Sermon by Saint Bernard of Clairvaux," CSQ 36, no. 3 (2001): 317–24.

Content

This sermon focuses on the monastic life, and therefore it is often viewed as one of Bernard's "monastic works," grouped together with works such as the *Apology to Abbot William*, *On Precept and Dispensation*, and Letters 1–12.[116] The opening line of the sermon, quoting Peter's words to Jesus from Matthew 19:27, sets the tone for the sermon and its most significant theme. He addresses the claim throughout the sermon, but now the monks are the audience instead of the disciples. The passage from Matthew is part of the larger story of the wealthy young man, who asks Jesus to tell him what he must do enter heaven and to whom Jesus responds that he must sell his possessions and give the proceeds to the poor. The key to this biblical passage is the point emphasized throughout the sermon: just as the young man in the story was told to go and sell all that he had, so too must the monks, searching inside themselves and reforming their conduct in order to follow Christ completely. As followers of Christ, Bernard says, monks have taken on "voluntary poverty" and also "contempt for the world," and these two charisms have filled the monasteries.[117] Bernard makes it clear that monastic profession requires the dedication of the whole person, that is, giving oneself over completely to God, both soul and body. This was the example of Christ, only possible after the incarnation. Before that, the "fathers of ancient times" were only able to devote themselves under one aspect, the spirit.

A discussion concerning the meaning of *regeneration* in Matthew 19:28 follows that point.[118] But Bernard makes no mention of the biblical text, instead moving to a discussion of the ontological reality of the body, soul, sin, and regeneration. Baptism is assumed here, but more than baptism is required, he says: one must also be born a second

[116] See Raciti's introduction to this sermon, "Pour la fête de saint Benoît," SCh 526:162–63. Other works of Bernard included in the volume's "monastic works" are also listed there and discussed.

[117] "Pour la fête de saint Benoît," SCh 526:174: *Haec sunt enim verba voluntariae persuasoria paupertatis et contemptus saeculi*.

[118] Based on the Vulgate Latin, the sermon here reads, "Amen, I say to you when the Son of Man sits on the throne of his majesty, you who have followed me in the regeneration will also sit on the twelve thrones, judging."

and a third time. The second birth is the restoration of the human soul, while the third is the resurrection of the body. Bernard's reference to this second birth here refers to those who are part of the monastic life, a theme Bernard included in *On Precept and Dispensation*.[119] His hope is that the monks who have gone through this second birth, which entails humility and a reformation of the heart, will eventually share in the third, their own bodily resurrection.[120]

The sermon then moves to the discussion of what one must do to progress toward God. Focusing on a different part of the same passage from Matthew 19:28, "when I sit you will also sit," Bernard encourages his monks to run, run after Christ, pursuing him without stopping and without sitting down. Avoid chasing "vain glory" (*vanam . . . gloriam*), he says, and do not seek pleasure, which is fleeting; spiritual labor should be embraced, for it has a sure reward.[121] These words echo themes from the first part of the sermon, such as the importance of obedience and relinquishing self-will (*voluntas propria*), which can hold dominion over a person, driving and badgering like a "cruel mistress" (*crudelis domina*).[122] The monks must dedicate themselves completely to their profession, turning their backs on the world: "Let them hold nothing back for themselves and nothing for others." The reward for this will be hundredfold and will lead to eternal life, the possession of "the homeland for our happiness."[123] The hundredfold, however, precedes the final reward and helps one along the journey with the first

[119] SBOp 3:288–89. In chapter 54 of this work, Bernard wrote of monastic profession as a second baptism.

[120] Bernard, "Pour la fête de saint Benoît," SCh 526:180, 182.

[121] Bernard, "Pour la fête de Saint Benoît," SCh 526:186, 188.

[122] Bernard, "Pour la fête de Saint Benoît," SCh 526:176. Cf. Pasc 3 (SBOp 5:105). The danger of self-will (*propria voluntas*) appears prominently in Bernard's Pasc 3, "Concerning Naaman's Leprosy." This sermon describes the double leprosy of the heart, that is, self-will, which is followed by something even more pernicious: exclusively relying on one's own counsel (*proprium consilium*). This proclivity stands in opposition, Bernard says, to the common will (*voluntas communis*). See also Lane, *Bernard of Clairvaux*, 223.

[123] Bernard, "Pour la fête de saint Benoît," SCh 526:194: *illa vero ad beatitudinem in patria possidebitur in aeternum*.

fruits of the Spirit, which visit and console the believer and are "sweeter than honey" (Ps 18:11).[124] These fruits are also "the testimony of our conscience . . . the memory of the abundance of God's sweetness . . . the great wealth of sweetness he keeps hidden for those who love him."[125]

In the final part of the sermon, in the penultimate sentence of the text, Bernard presents the reader with a surprise. Raciti has uncovered a cryptogram embedded in the Latin text. The number of syllables in each segment or "verse" varies, but the total number of syllables added together equals 91. When the number is written in Roman numerals, it is XCI, closely resembling the first three letters of *Christ Jesus* in Greek.[126] New insights can come unexpectedly, but none is more welcome than another of Bernard's sermons.

❖ ❖ ❖

In 1970, just fifty years ago, Cistercian Publications published the first volume of Saint Bernard's works in English, with *Apologia to Abbot William*; *On Precept and Dispensation*; *The Prologue to the Cistercian Antiphonary*; and *The Office of St Victor*, respectively translated by Michael Casey, Conrad Greenia, Chrysogonus Waddell, and Martinus Cawley, all members of the Cistercian Order of the Strict Observance (OCSO). It was categorized as Bernard of Clairvaux, *Treatises I*, in The Works of Bernard of Clairvaux volume 1, Cistercian Fathers Series number 1.

Now this final small volume of Bernard's "Various Sermons" completes the English translation of the works of Bernard of Clairvaux that began fifty years ago. We celebrate its appearance.

[124] See Rom 8:23 (NRSV), "and not only the creation, but we ourselves, who have the first fruits of the Spirit, groan inwardly while we wait for adoption, the redemption of our bodies."

[125] Bernard, "Pour la fête de saint Benoît," SCh 526:196.

[126] See Raciti's introduction in *Sermons variés*, SCh 526:171. Raciti's analysis of the sentence lists it section by section in a helpful chart with the number of syllables in each phrase listed to the right of each portion of text. The chart also appears in Raciti's "Un nouveau sermon," 97.

Sermons

Sermon One

For Advent: On the Three Realms of the Dead[1]

1. During the celebration of the Lord's coming, our reading and singing bring to memory the desires our holy fathers had, those men whom God honored with a revelation through the Holy Spirit of the redemption that was to come through his Son, who would become flesh and die for the salvation of humankind. Some of these men, while still in the flesh, foresaw the incarnation of Christ by a spirit of prophecy and left behind for us in their writings the deep inner joy they had conceived and the ardor of their longing. Once they had been released from the

[1] *de triplici inferno.* The word *infernus,* literally "what lies beneath," was used both to refer to the concept of a neutral underworld where the dead dwelt (the concept of *Sheol* in the Old Testament or *Hades* in Greek thought) and the punitive region of hell as it was understood by Christian writers. Because the word *hell* contains strong connotations of torment that are not necessarily implied by the word *infernus,* as well as a specific vision of the afterlife not proper to the context, it is an imperfect word for translation here. In this sermon Bernard uses *infernus* to refer not only to hell, but also to purgatory and to the "netherworld" of religious life. Therefore I have used a variety of words to translate *infernus,* including *Sheol, hell, netherworld, land,* or *realm of the dead,* and in a few instances simply *realm.*

flesh and were sitting in Sheol, *sitting in darkness and the shadow of death*,* it is impossible easily to express or imagine the great desire with which they awaited the one who alone was able to remove the yoke of their captivity.

*Luke 1:79

We should take a lesson from their desire and learn how much we should long and sigh as we wait in this body of death, in the Sheol of this darkness, for the coming of our Redeemer, so he will come frequently to console us in this prison and ultimately lead us out of it. We must understand that before Christ's coming the holy fathers, or rather all people, the good as well as the bad, descended into the land of the dead, although they occupied vastly different places there according to the difference of their merits. They descended there because of the transgression of the first human being, who earned exile from Paradise with a taste of forbidden fruit. This sin caused not only him but all of his descendants as well to be cast into this exile, where, driven by that original sin, we thirst, we hunger, we feel the cold, we grow weak, and ultimately we die.

2. During this exile, dear brothers, we must give thorough consideration to what a grievous fall may be awaiting us because of our own sins—those sins by which we offend God knowingly and with pleasure—when a sin to which we never gave our assent caused us to plummet into such misery. If the sin of another has banished us from Paradise into this world where we are pierced by so many thorns of such terrible misery, where will we fall to because of our own sins? To hell, most certainly, where truly there is no redemption.

Just as it was not our own fault but another's that cast us into this prison, so also it was not our own offering of reparation but another's that provided a way out for us again. For *just as through Adam all die, so through Christ all will be made alive*.* If, however, we are banished into hell on account of our own transgressions, there is no

*1 Cor 15:22

hope of recovery left, because *Christ rising from the dead now dies no more*,* and he will certainly not descend again into the land of the dead to plunder it. We should also note that even though Adam sinned right away he was not immediately expelled, but the Lord, wishing to wrest a confession from him, asked, *Adam, where are you?** The one who gave the commandment not to sin prescribed the remedy of confession to the repentant. Not everyone who sins is excluded from the kingdom of God, therefore, but only those who after sinning fall into contempt.

*Rom 6:9

*Gen 3:9

Ultimately, eating the fruit was not such a big thing, but God had placed Adam in his own household, where he wanted there to be no disobedience. This is why, whether the matter was something little or something great, Adam deserved expulsion: because he was disobedient without being contrite.[2] The same is true with you; as long as you were in the world you were outside the household of God; for *my kingdom*, he says, *is not of this world*.* Many things were permissible for you there—things you could say or do—that now that you have been set in the household of God are considered sins if you show contempt for the observances regarding them or do not wash away that contempt with tears of repentance.

*John 18:36

3. We said that before Christ's coming everyone descended into the land of the dead on account of the original sin. But we can also say, and with equal veracity, that there is not a single person—whether before his coming or after—who does not first descend into the land of the dead before ascending into heaven, because there are in fact three realms of the dead.

[2] The idea that Adam and Eve's refusal to confess was the real reason for their expulsion from Paradise occurs several places in Bernard's writings. See Pre 27, Ann 1.8, and OS 1.3.

**consumptionis*

*Mark 9:43

*John 5:24
‡*propriis voluptatibus*
†Col 3:5

*Heb 11:25

One is the netherworld of destruction,* where there is the worm that never dies and the fire that never goes out.* There is no redemption there. Another is the netherworld of expiation, which is the destination of souls that need to be purified after death. Another is the netherworld of affliction or, in other words, voluntary poverty. As people who have renounced the world, we should by means of voluntary poverty afflict our souls for the sake of our healing, so that when we die we do not pass into Judgment, but pass from death to life.* In this netherworld are all who renounce the selfish gratifications‡ of the flesh by suitable penance and so *put to death their earthly members,*† *choosing to be afflicted with the people of God rather than to have the fleeting enjoyment of sin.** Those who do not take the trouble to descend into this realm while still in the flesh will someday descend into one of the other two. They will narrowly find redemption if they find it at all.

*Matt 5:26

The first realm is exacting[3] because in that place payment is required *to the last penny*,* and so its punishment is unending. Where nothing is forgiven, there is no end to the demand for a payment able to requite the wrong done to God. It is such a terrible thing to insult the Creator by disobedience that no punishment can expiate it unless God first offers his forgiveness. We see this clearly in the first transgression: because of it even babies, who have nothing to be forgiven for in baptism, are eternally damned.

The second realm is purifying. The third realm is absolving. Because the third netherworld is voluntary, often both punishment and guilt are absolved there. In the second netherworld, on the other hand, even though punishment is sometimes absolved, guilt never is, but

[3] *exactorius.* The literal meaning of the word is to have the character of a person who extracts, extorts, or demands payment, such as a tax collector.

the guilt that had previously been absolved is now washed away. O happy netherworld of poverty in which Christ was born and nurtured and led his life while he dwelt in the flesh! Into this realm he descended not only once in order to bring out those who were his own, but *he who gave himself so that he might deliver us from this present evil age** continues to gather there with those whom he sets apart from the multitude of the lost until the time comes for him to bring them out. *Gal 1:4

In this realm are found the young maidens,[4] souls just starting out, yes, *girls playing their timbrels*,* with *the princes*, the angels, *going before them clanging their cymbals* as they follow after *with cymbals of joy*.* In the other realms people are tormented, but in this realm it is the demons who are now tormented. They roam through dry and parched places, seeking rest and not finding it. Yes, circling around in the minds of the faithful, they are shoved and driven out from every side by holy meditations and prayers. And so with good reason they cry out, *Jesus, why have you come to torment us before the time?** *Ps 67:26 *Ps 150:5 *Matt 8:29

They also have their own netherworld, those pleasure seekers who make themselves comfortable in the world and *make* as much *provision for the desires of the flesh** as they can. Yes, they have their hell, I say, a hell in which they are tormented even in the midst of pleasure. They do not notice, however, since they are asleep and drunk with wine, with a lethal love of the world, that is, with *the incurable venom of the asp*.* A person bitten by the asp falls asleep and dies. Yes, *intoxicated with wormwood*,* with the wretched, bitter sweetness of the world, these people grow forgetful of God* and themselves; they are *a people without sense and without* knowledge, *not understanding or giving thought to the last things*.* *When* *Rom 13:14 *Deut 32:33 *Lam 3:15 *Ps 9:18 *Deut 32:28-29

[4] *adoscentulae*, the word that is used for the young maidens in the Song of Songs 1:2; 1:3; 6:7.

*they say "peace and security," then sudden destruction will come upon them and pain as that which comes upon a pregnant woman, and they will not escape.**

*1 Thess 5:3

4. Blessed be God that *we are not in darkness, for the day of the Lord to catch us** unprepared, because *God has not destined us for wrath,** like those who live without sense in the world, who accumulate sins and *store up wrath for themselves on the day when the just judgment of God will be revealed,** but *God has destined us to obtain salvation** *as we redeem the time*‡ that is ours by making a proper satisfaction of penance. Carnal people, on the other hand, find the source of their torment in the very things that delight them; what they have is not enough for them, but they thirst for what they do not have. They will often experience what it is to grow disgusted with something, but they will never experience what it is to be satisfied, since they know only how to glory in vile and despicable miseries.

*1 Thess 5:4
*1 Thess 5:9
*Rom 2:5
*1 Thess 5:9
‡Eph 5:16

Those who have removed themselves from the world, *who chastise their bodies and reduce them to slavery,** are not the only ones to drink from the cup of the passion, for *the Lord holds in his hand a cup filled with pure wine, of mixed wine, a cup not drained of its dregs*, and *all the sinners on the earth will drink* from it.* The cup represents the passion, and so he says, *Can you drink the cup which I will drink?** This cup is in the hand of the Lord, it is held in his power, because he offers it to whom he wants, when he wants, offering from it what he wants.

*1 Cor 9:27
*Ps 74:9
*Matt 20:22

Some people drink pure wine from this cup, namely those who *renounce themselves* for the Lord alone and, *taking up their cross, follow* him.* Some drink mixed wine from the cup. These are people who have entered upon the way of poverty, but without fully renouncing themselves or their parents. A sort of animal attachment* causes them to continue to feel responsibility for their parents or to devote themselves to excessive care for the flesh. It is still wine that they drink, however, although

*Matt. 16:24
**animali affectu*

it is mixed, because even if they are not perfect they have not thrown off the yoke of obedience.

But those people drink the dregs who, in order to sate the desires of the flesh, endure the pain and weariness with which the world abounds, dissipated into *vanities and senseless follies*.* Every moment of their life is spent in the dregs and disgrace that the prophet reproaches when he says, *drink and go to sleep; the cup of the Lord's right hand will envelop you and the vomit of shame will cover your glory*.* Yes, these people drink, suffering miseries far more grievous than those which Christ's poor ones seem to suffer. Even their glory is all so shameful that anyone in their right mind thrusts it aside like a cloth stained with vomit. Such people drink a cup of pestilence and not *the cup of salvation*, because they do not *call upon the name of the Lord*.* Yes indeed, *let them forsake wickedness, all who call upon the name of the Lord!** Without a doubt, *whoever calls upon the name of the Lord will be saved*.*

*Ps 39:5 *Hab 2:16 *Ps 115:13 *2 Tim 2:19 *Acts 2:21

5. In the netherworld of poverty—to leave aside the others—the city of God *is on sojourn, away from the Lord so long as it is in the body*.* It is a holy city, yes, a beautiful city in spite of being set *in a place of affliction*.* The bridegroom praises its beauty in the Song, saying, *you are beautiful, my love, sweet and lovely as Jerusalem, terrible as a regiment of troops drawn up for battle*.* To the people it is sweet, to the heavenly beings it is lovely, and to the demons it is terrible. Why? Because it marches on like a regiment of troops, not scattered about by envy but drawn together in close ranks by charity. It is a regiment because it is a gathering, troops because girded for battle, drawn up in formation because of its unanimity. Repentance produces the gathering, watchfulness does the arming, a union of hearts* furnishes the unanimity.[5]

*2 Cor 5:6 *Ps 43:20 *Song 6:3 **concordia*

[5] *Acies est per conventum, castrorum per procinctum, ordinate per consensum. Conventum facit paenitentia, procinctum ponit vigilantia, consensum praebet concordia.*

The devil has little fear of those who fast, those who keep vigil, or those who practice continence. After all, he has drawn as many of one as of the other into *the snare of ruin.** But those with one heart, living in harmony in the house of the Lord, united to God and to one another by the bond of love—these bring pain, fear, and envy* upon the devil. This oneness of the many not only torments the enemy but also wins over God, as he himself testifies in the Song: *you have wounded my heart my sister, my bride, with one of your eyes and with one lock of your hair.** That is to say, by the unity of superiors and those under them.[6] This is why Paul gives the warning, *be careful to preserve the unity of spirit in the bond of peace.**

*Hos 9:8

**livorem*

*Song 4:9

*Eph 4:3

The evil spirit knows well that the Son does not lose any of those whom the Father has given him,* for *there is no one who can pluck them from* his *hand.** When the devil finds people who are of one heart, by this in particular he recognizes *that they are in the hand of God and the torment of death will not touch them.** The Lord said, *by this all will know*, even the demons, *that you are my disciples, if you have love for one another.** Love between people, that is what terrifies the devil, the love that he could not keep in heaven with God and the angels. Love is the firm and unshakable city.

*John 18:9

*Deut 32:39

*Wis 3:1

*John 13:35

Her *neck is like the tower of David, built with battlements. A thousand shields hang from it, all the armaments of the strong.** The neck joins the head to the body, so what better meaning can be given to the neck than our resolve?[7] As long as it remains intact, no matter how

*Song 4:4

[6] *Praelatorum et subditorum.* The word *praelatorum* refers not only to abbots, but to any of those who hold high rank or office in the monastery.

[7] *Propositum.* This word can have the specific meaning of a commitment to the monastic way of life, or even to a particular community.

many tribulations afflict us we are never separated from our head, Christ. *We suffer tribulation in every way, but we are not distressed.** For *who will separate us from the love* of God,* the love that causes us *to run the way of God's commandments with expanded hearts*?* The neck should therefore be firm and unmoving, rising up like a tower, and its foundation must be humility.

*2 Cor 4:8

*Rom 8:35

*Ps 118:32; RB Prol. 49

6. It is this tower that gathers the virtues together, preserves what is gathered, and perfects what is preserved. The foundation lies in the earth, and its weakness cannot be detected until the walls that have been built upon it begin to lean or to crumble. It is the same with humility; it sinks its root into the secret places of the heart, and the absence or fragility of this root cannot be known until the wall of the building starts to buckle as it falls out of line, or collapses altogether when it splits.[8]

This tower belongs to David, the man with a strong hand.* If you are not a contemplative, do not despair! Be active, devote yourself to good works, and by strongly defending the tower of your resolve you will one day arrive at purity of heart. God handed himself over *so that he might redeem us from all iniquity and purify for himself an acceptable people, doers of good works.** Accordingly, he swore to David, to the one who acts with strength, *the fruit of your womb*—of your sensuality, that is, which is the most delicate part of the human person—*I will set upon your throne.**

**manu fortis*; Jerome, *Inter* 53; PL 23:813

*Titus 2:14

*Ps 131:11

This tower or city has obedience for a wall, which gathers those who are scattered and reigns in the wandering so that they do not go out except through the door, except, that is, by the order of the superior.* Obedience has five aspects. The first is acting uprightly, because there is no such thing as obedience that goes

**prioris*

[8] *donec murus aedificii vel fundatur per exordinationem vel omnino corruat per separationem.*

against God. The second is acting voluntarily, because what is done out of compulsion is not good. The third is acting in purity, with a pure intention, because *if the eye is simple, the whole body is full of light.** The fourth is acting with discretion so that nothing is done to excess, for *the one who offers rightly, if he does not discriminate rightly, sins.*[9]* The fifth aspect is firmness of action, in other words persevering, and this aspect of obedience includes and keeps all the rest. After all, nothing is good without perseverance. In order for the wall of obedience to have perseverance, however, it must be attached to the battlements of patience. Just as those who are defending a wall need battlements to guard themselves from the enemy's arrows, those who want to hold fast to obedience need patience, which protects a person from being upset by hurtful words and tiring tasks.[10]

*Matt 6:22

*Gen 4:7 LXX

7. *A thousand shields hang from this tower:** perfect and continual prayer. This prayer sometimes goes to a neighbor's aid, for a shield can be carried around from place to place. From this tower hang *all the armaments of the strong.** Let Paul come and explain: *Furthermore, take up the armor of God, so that you can withstand the devil's attacks and stand perfect in everything. Stand therefore, your loins girt with the truth, and put on the cuirass*[11] *of justice, your feet shod with readiness for the gospel of peace, taking up the shield of faith in all circumstances,** and the rest. To gird your loins means simply to abstain from the desires of the flesh, but truth must be the belt. Some

*Song 4:4

*Song 4:4

*Eph 6:11, 13-16

[9] *Qui recte offert, si non recte dividit, peccat.* In this reading of Genesis, Cain's fault was that while he made his offering to God, he did not offer the best of what he had. Bernard likens this to doing things with the right intention, but without good judgment.

[10] *Quae munit hominem contra verborum acerbitates et operum fatigationes.*

[11] A cuirass is a piece of armor that covers the entire torso. Although the Latin word, *lorica*, can mean *breast plate*, it is clear from what follows that Bernard is envisioning the more general meaning of the word.

people are continent out of necessity, not having the place, time, or means of opportunity. Some people are continent out of vanity, in order to win the good opinion of others or to gain some temporal advantage. Some people are continent out of truth, desiring to please God alone.

We must also put on the cuirass of justice. A cuirass protects a person in front and behind, from those on the right and those on the left. It is right to liken it to justice, which gives to everyone what is theirs, for we have seniors before us, juniors behind us, friends on our right, and enemies on our left. Let us give to all of them what belongs to them: obedience to seniors, instruction to juniors, cheerfulness to friends, and patience to enemies.

8. We must also shoe our feet with readiness for the Gospel of peace. In order to proclaim peace to others and to keep peace with others we must put shoes on the feet of our thoughts. We travel over the whole world with these feet, and they must be shod with the memory of our dead works to prevent the thorn of pride from piercing us when we notice our neighbors' weaknesses. In order to keep us from setting ourselves above our neighbors when we think about our weakness and theirs, we should not drive away the memory of our own sins, even if in our consciences they are dead, reflecting on the apostle's words: *examining yourself, lest you also be tempted.** When such thoughts come *Gal 6:1
upon us, therefore, we should accuse ourselves and excuse our neighbor, so that, having executed justice by giving to all what belongs to them, we may now execute judgment. Then the soul, which ought to be the throne of God, may be set right by justice and judgment, because *justice and judgment are the setting of his throne.** *Ps 96:2

Judgment is threefold. Judgment is one thing towards oneself, another towards one's neighbor, and yet another towards God. A person's judgment should be

**pium* severe towards oneself, merciful* towards one's neighbor, and pure towards God. We should judge ourselves
*1 Cor 11:31 severely, for *if we judge ourselves, we will not be judged.** You should judge a neighbor with mercy so that whether you are imploring with compassion or rebuking out of zeal, you do both *in a spirit of gentleness, examining yourself*
*Gal 6:1 *lest you also be tempted.** You should reflect on God's judgments in purity and simplicity of heart, *confessing*
*Sir 39:21 *with your lips that all the works of the Lord are very good.** May we be demanding judges of ourselves because we know the truth, merciful judges of our neighbors be-
**affectum* cause we have the affection* of love, and pure judges of God through the assent of our will.

9. After executing justice and judgment, we need vigilance in order to avoid growing lax through tepidity or sinking into ruin through self-conceit. It is good for
*Mic 6:8 people *to walk conscientiously with* their *God,** being subject to him and praying to him. But lest we grow listless
**haesitat* in prayer or become paralyzed* by the devil's hidden and malevolent suggestions, let us take up the shield of faith in all circumstances, knowing that *wherever the foot*
*Deut 11:24 of our faith *treads, the place will belong to* us.* In other words, whatever we ask of God or in his name will be
John 14:13 done for us.

Luke 17:6 May your faith, therefore, be like a grain of mustard, which the more it is ground the more it gives off its aroma. However much you seem to be ignored or rebuffed by your God, you may all the more confidently hope to wrest from him what you ask, because *even if he does not do it because* you *are his friend, nevertheless he will arise because of* your *importunity and give* you *whatever*
*Luke 11:8 *you need.** This is why the apostle concludes with the words *praying in the spirit and keeping watch in the same*
*Eph 6:18 *spirit, with all constancy and supplication.** We must not approach God just once or twice in prayer, but frequently and continually, holding out to God the desires
*Ps 31:6 of our hearts and, *at a suitable time,** lifting up the sound

of our voices.[12] This is why the apostle says elsewhere, *let your petitions be made known to God,** because it is frequency and constancy of prayer, addressed now to him, now to his glorious mother, now to the saints, that drives them to say, *send* him *away, for* he *is crying after us.**

*Phil 4:6

*Matt 15:23

10. The prophet therefore consoles the holy city of Jerusalem, still on pilgrimage in the hell of poverty, with the words *do not weep, for soon your salvation will come.** For *by the rivers of Babylon, there we sat and wept.*‡ *Babylon* is confusion.[13] In Babylon the citizens of Jerusalem sit and weep. Even if their deeds are not confused, nevertheless they are confused in their thoughts, wanting but unable to direct the mind's eye to God while worthless things draw them away against their will. The rivers of Babylon, therefore, are perverse habits. They run sweet in our memory, but nevertheless they run, and those whom they carry off they carry with them into the sea that is the world. Willows spring up along these rivers, feeble and unfruitful thoughts. Upon them, so long as we are distracted by worthless things, we hang up our hearts, suspending them from the praise of God when, being the instruments of praise, they should be resounding in God's presence. But *thanks be to God who has given us the victory through our Lord Jesus Christ.** Even if bad habits make their way in, we do not settle ourselves *upon* them, but we sit *beside* the rivers of Babylon, because when the sweetness of worldly life spoke to our souls, they remained silent, when it called them to return they turned a deaf ear,[14] and when it tried to charm them with flattery, they hardened against it.

*Response for 2nd Nocturn of the 1st Sunday of Advent, which begins "City of Jerusalem"; see Tobit 5:26
‡Ps 136:1

*1 Cor 15:57

[12] *Ad Deum extendentes desideria cordis et in tempore opportune aperientes vocem oris.*

[13] Jerome, *Interpretatio* 106 (PL 23:851).

[14] *Obsorduit.* Normally this would be a form of the verb *obsordesco*, "to get dirty or wear out," but it seems more likely that Bernard

Ensnared by all these vanities, it is not surprising if *we weep remembering Zion*, or in other words, when we recall the sweetness and the pleasure of that flavor of
speculatores which those watchmen get a foretaste, those who have
*2 Cor 3:18 merited *to look upon the glory of God with unveiled faces.** *Unhappy man that I am, who will free me from the yoke of*
*Rom 7:24 *this slavery,** so that I may one day taunt my enemies who now taunt me? Because my sins demanded it, God
*Ps 43:14 *has made me an object of scorn and derision** to them, *humbling me in the place of affliction,* where *the shadow of*
*Ps 43:20 *death covers me.** After all, if I am drawn by the desires of the flesh, and, God forbid, I consent to them, I am in death as much as I can be. Yes, I am dead and will as a consequence be buried in hell.* If, however, I feel
*Luke 16:22 their assault but withhold my consent, I am not in death, but I am in the shadow of death. I am in the shadow of death so long as the dust of vain thoughts dims my eyes and my memory summons me away from the sweetness of my God. And yet, *if I walk in the midst of the shadow of death I will have no fear of evil* if *you are with me*, or no, rather, *I will have no fear, for you are with*
*Ps 22:4 *me.**

11. And where do I dare to get such a hope? The rod of your correction and the staff of your support, *these*
*Ps 22:4 *things console me.** Even if you correct me and curb my
*Job 10:9 pride, *returning me to the dust of death,** you still nurture my life, supporting me lest I sink into the pit of death. I will *not neglect the discipline of the Lord*, nor will I be
*Heb 12:5 indignant *when he rebukes me.** *I know that all things work*
*Rom 8:28 *for good for those who love God.**

Yes, *the creature has been made subject to vanity, not of its*
*Rom 8:20 *own will** but in sorrow.‡ Is the creature impatient, then?
‡*non volens sed dolens* No, but it bears up patiently. Why? *Because of the one*
†Rom 8:20 *who subjected it in hope.*† Why? So *that the creature itself*

---

was thinking of the word *obsurdesco*, "to become deaf." The French translation in Sources Chrétiennes takes this interpretation.

*will also be set free from its bondage to corruption and enter into the freedom of the glory of the children of God.** So *do not weep, city of Jerusalem, for soon your salvation will come.** If he seems to you to delay, he will not be slow as far as he is concerned,‡ *because in his sight a thousand years are as yesterday which has come and gone.*†

*Rom 8:21

*Response for 2nd Nocturn of the 1st Sunday of Advent, which begins "City of Jerusalem"; see Tobit 5:26

‡Hab 2:3

†Ps 89:4

Sermon Two

For Epiphany

1. Our holy fathers handed down to us a threefold reason for this feast, as we all know. On this day a new star, indicating the new birth of a king, led three magi from the east to adore the Christ in Bethlehem. Offering mystic gifts, they confessed him to be king with gold, God with incense,
Matt 2:1-11 man with myrrh. On this day, in his thirtieth year, Christ Jesus came to John the Baptist and, *in order to*
*Matt 3:15 *fulfill all justice*,* placed himself under him. This was not a lesser submitting to a greater, not an equal to an equal, but a greater to a lesser. The Lord was baptized by a servant, the master by a disciple, the maker by his handiwork, the pure by the impure, God by man. One year later, on this same day it is believed, he turned water
John 2:9 into wine when he called John the Evangelist, who was preparing to marry, away from his wedding,[1] mani-
John 2:11 festing his glory with this miracle.

[1] The identification of the bridegroom at Cana as John the disciple, called away from his bride by Jesus before the marriage was consummated, was popular during the Middle Ages. The first-known source for this legend is a revised version of *De ortu et orbitu patrum* by Ps-Isidore, which appears in Ireland around 750. In the early twelfth century Rupert of Deutz wrote that it was an opinion held by "nearly everyone," *ipsius istas fuisse nuptias, opinio fere omnium est* (PL 169:284). For a fuller discussion of this tradition, see Annette Volfing, *John the Evangelist in Medieval German Writing: Imitating the Inimitable* (Oxford: Oxford University Press, 2001), 27–31.

Therefore this solemnity is called *Epiphany*, that is, "appearance from above."[2] It is called this not because the Son of God first appeared on earth on this day, but because just as he showed himself to be true man on the day of his birth by being born, by crying, and by suffering all the other frailties of human life, so the sacred signs of such great mysteries proved on this day that he was true God. Would a new star have been created for the birth of a human being, causing someone merely human to be adored and given such gifts? When he was baptized, what could have more clearly declared his divinity than the heavens' opening above him and the voice of the Father ringing out, bearing witness to him, saying, *this is my beloved Son in whom I am well pleased*?* Again, when he manifested his glory by causing water to become wine, was he not openly teaching that he is God? It was then that *his disciples* first *came to believe in him.**

*Matt 3:17

*John 2:11

2. Having touched upon these things, let us see if we can draw a moral teaching from the great depth of these mysteries. We need three things in order to return to our homeland: the will, the ability, and the knowledge. After all, without the *will*, we would never *carry out a good desire.** On the other hand, what good is it to have the will to return if we lack the ability to do so? Then again, if your will has ability for a companion but you do not know the most direct way, you could experience all the hardships of the journey but never have the joy of arriving at the destination. You need the will to rouse you, the flesh to act, and the reason to guide you. These powers of the soul were conferred on you at creation. Yes, they are natural, but they are completely useless unless grace next comes to put them in order and remains with them to the end. And so it

*Phil 2:13

[2] *Supra apparitio*, a literal Latin translation of the Greek word ἐπιφάνεια (*epiphania*).

is up to the reason to make judgments, the will to give assent, and the body to offer its service. When aided by grace, the reason's judgments are clear-sighted, the will's
pia desire is healthy, and the body's service is loyal.

But when the devil enters our souls through fleshly desires and worldly allurements and sets up his throne there, he clouds the reason's judgment, he perverts the will's desire, and he misdirects the flesh's service. Truly
*Ps 9:28 *his mouth is full of cursing, bitterness, and deceit.** For at the beginning of his creation, when the devil should have sought to increase his blessing, he, glorying in his uniqueness, rushed into the fullness of a curse. When he should have risen through grace from being able to avoid sin to being unable to sin, his innate pride drove him to descend into being unable to avoid sin. I said it well when I said that he rushed into the fullness of a curse since he delights in it, acts on it, and glories in it. This is why the psalm says that a curse penetrates *like*
*Ps 108:18 *oil into a person's bones;** this is to delight in evil. It is *like*
*Ps 108:18 *a garment which he puts on;** this is to commit evil. What
*Ps 108:19 is more, it becomes *like a garment which covers him;** this is to glory in a curse.

The Son *willed to give us birth by the word of truth, so*
*Jas 1:18 *that we might be a sort of beginning of his creatures,** *new*
*2 Cor 5:17 *creatures in Christ,** walking not in the old ways of the
*Rom 6:4; Rom 7:6 flesh but *walking in the newness of the Spirit.**

3. The devil wanted us to be corrupted at the beginning of our creation just as he was corrupted at the beginning of his creation, so that we would exchange our blessing for a curse. He wanted us to share with him not only the inability to avoid sin, but even to make us share his inability to repent.[3] Though we did at one time incur a curse, from which came our original

[3] *quatenus sicut commune habemus cum ipso non posse non peccare, ita et nobis communicet non posse paenitere.*

inability to avoid sin, it was not the fullness of the curse, because we do have the ability to repent.

And so, at the beginning of your rebirth the devil speaks to you not of the sweetness of religious life but of its bitterness in order to get you to join with him in his curse. He enumerates the painful aspects of the monastic rule* on the one hand, and the enjoyments of the world on the other. With a certain evil craftiness he stems the fear of future torments while he stokes the fear of present ones. Whether he is describing the sweetness of the world or the bitterness of religious life, his intention is to deceive, because even though he has put on the hat of compassion and seems to express plenty of heartfelt concern for your frailty, his aim is only to get you to bask in the moment and be tormented for eternity. **ordinis tormenta*

With great skill and spite the devil often confuses the reason with his deceitful assertions, making its judgment grow blind or reckless. Moreover, *under his tongue are toil and pain,** since the flesh wearies with toil while employed in wild carousing, and the will is racked with pain as long as it is steeped in carnal desires and cannot carry out what it intends. And so, with reason's judgment confused, the will's desire perverted, and the flesh employed in carousing, *the well-armed strong man*, the devil, *guards the house* of the will, and *while he does so, what he possesses is in peace.** *A triple cord is hard to break,*‡ and now that the will is in charge, captive reason decides as the will directs and unbridled flesh obeys. *Ps 9:28 *Luke 11:21 ‡Eccl 4:12

*At the favorable time** our loving‡ Lord knocks at the door of your heart with his gracious goodness, because *he has saved us not because of any works of righteousness that we have done but according to his mercy.** Right away reason hears him knocking, but, being alone, it is unable to open the door. It gives the will a knock but finds it dead, choked with the poison of worldly pleasure. Reason gives the body* a knock, too, and finds it crazed. *Ps 31:6 ‡*pius* *Titus 3:5 **sensualitatem*

Through the action of grace, however, reason manages to prod the body to life and sends it to welcome the one who is knocking, while the will screams in protest.

This is why it says, *where two or three are gathered in my name, there am I in their midst.** Three are gathered in the name of the Lord when the will, the reason, and the flesh unite for the good. Again, *a triple cord is hard to break.** Two are gathered when reason, enlightened by grace, makes the flesh serve even if it cannot change the will. But as long as the will is opposed to these two, there is no peace within. Reason chooses, and the flesh does what the will does not like. Yet when the two sisters pray for Lazarus,* the will is healed and peace is established.

*Matt 18:20

*Eccl 4:12

*John 11:3

*Eph 2:14

4. And so, to the Son of God, who *is our peace,** reason offers the gold of devotion, the will offers the incense of prayer, and the flesh offers the myrrh of mortification—incense to God, gold to the king, myrrh to the man.

The Son of God was to reconcile the heights with the depths, and so he needed to come to know the weakness of humanity just as he knew the power of divinity. Therefore, what he knew from all eternity by knowledge, he learned more intimately in time by experience[4] when he became man, *mounting a light cloud,** or, in other words, assuming flesh free from every stain of sin. This flesh was a cloud in comparison with the splendor of his majesty, but completely light with respect to the weight of our corruption. In this flesh he was so touched by torments, even though it was not subject to sin, that in the end he sweated blood* and *was sorrowful unto death.**

*Isa 19:1

*Luke 22:44

*Matt 26:38

[4] *Necesse habuit ut infirmitatem cognosceret humanitatis, sicut et potentiam noverat divinitatis. Quod ergo noverat ab aeterno per scientiam, factus homo tempore familiarius didicit per experientiam.*

He knew human misery as true man and the justice of God as God. Humanity had no means to offer a worthy payment for procuring forgiveness, and God had not discovered within his own hidden counsel a way to acquit guilt without proper satisfaction. O merciful and priceless Mediator, O *angel of great* and unsearchable *counsel*,* *who has known* your *mind or who was* *Isa 9:6
your *counselor?** You saw that mercy was on one side *Rom 11:34
and justice on the other, but you *worked your salvation in the middle*,* safeguarding justice but *exalting mercy* *Ps 73:12
above it.* *Jas 2:13

Yes, great was the opposition between God and humanity: God is immortal and true while humans, on the contrary, are mortal and false. Being the one who was to mediate between the two, the Son of God wanted to have something in common with them both; from humanity he took on mortality, and from the Father he took hold of the truth. He took on mortality so that he might know human misery; he held fast to the truth so that he might serve the Father's justice. He took on mortality so that he might experience and have compassion on our weakness; he held to the truth in order to please the Father more sweetly and to convey the mystery of the Redeemer more fully. Mediating between the mortal liar and the one who is immortal and true, he who was mortal but true had the counsel that would be of help to humanity and possessed the judgment needed to preserve the honor of the royal majesty. For truly, *the king's honor loves judgment*.* *Ps 98:4

5. And so, in accordance with the Father's command, he judged that humanity would be punished with death, but he counseled people to do penance to avoid punishment after death. On the one hand he was calling upon people to confess the truth, but on the other hand he was calling upon God, who is love,* to forgive in- *1 John 4:8
iquity, for *love rejoices in the truth*.* Thus he made it so *1 Cor 13:6
that in human life *mercy and truth have met*.* This did *Ps 84:11

not contradict God's sentence, because in death, which is unavoidable, human *righteousness and peace have kissed.* Before the incarnation of our Redeemer, God's censure was so severe that no one, however righteous, could find peace in God's sight whether in death or in life, because in life a person was subject to the passions of human corruption and in death the person descended into hell. But now, even though life's miseries are many, righteousness meets with peace in death. Why? Because for those who do penance, *the kingdom of heaven is near*
*Matt 3:2 *at hand*,* so when they die they pass from sorrow to joy.

Our Redeemer urged and persuaded[5] people to do penance, and in order that this penance might find peace in the sight of God's righteousness, the Son of God presented his very self as *a sweet smelling offering*
*Eph 5:2 *and sacrifice to God*,* *erasing* with his blood *the bond that*
*Col 2:15 *stood against us** and washing from us the stench of
see Gen 8:21 human corruption. The Father smelled and accepted
**pium* the new and filial* sacrifice of his only begotten. He no longer wished *to judge anyone, but gave all judgment*
*John 5:22 *to the Son*,* so now we breathe more easily in the hands of the man who suffered for us and with us, the one to
*Matt 28:18 whom *authority has been given in heaven and on earth.**

What then will separate us from his love? Tribulation,
*Rom 8:35 *anguish, persecution, famine, nakedness, danger, or sword?** Absolutely not, because he has authority on earth. What
*Rom 8:38 then? *Angels? Principalities? Powers*?* No indeed, because he has authority in heaven. Being *compassionate and*
*Ps 85:15 *merciful*,* our Mediator had pity on human beings, and being just, he also observed the Father's justice. This is why he descended from the towering throne of his majesty into the valley of our weakness, why he left his hidden solitude to come into our midst, left the tower-

[5] *suasit et persuasit.*

ing throne of his glory to enter into our unhappy exile, saying marvelous things in order to instruct us, working miracles in order to imprint faith in us, and suffering torments so that *he might communicate his love to us.** He visited humanity as both man and God so he might lead us from the man to God, from weakness to majesty, from misery to glory, from sadness to the joy that cannot be taken away from us.*

*Rom 5:8

*John 16:20, 22

6. He is man, God, and king: as man he reconciles, as God he pardons, as king he rules. Let us offer myrrh to the man by *carrying around his dying in our mortal flesh,** because we must be conformed to the image of his humanity now in this present time if we wish to be reformed to the image of his divinity, the image to which we were fashioned. Let us offer to God the incense of prayer, *sending up our prayer in his presence,** so that by the gift of his grace we might *be conformed to the image of his Son** in spirit as well as in flesh. To the king let us offer the gold of such devotion that whether our king and guide leads us by the broad road or the narrow way,* our devotion relishes his leadership and finds it so agreeable that we even *glory in our tribulations,** *counting it all as joy when we meet with various trials** and adversities. Why? Because *all things*, adversities as well as prosperities, *work for good for those who love God.**

*2 Cor 4:10-11

*Ps 140:2

*Rom 8:29

*Matt 7:13-14

*Rom 5:3

*Jas 1:2

*Rom 8:28

Gold signifies wisdom in the Scriptures. Wisdom gets its name from taste,[6] and where there is a taste for something there is devotion. You remain devout in those things in which you relish God. Gold is a precious reward, and the taste for good is a precious acquisition. *What* then *will separate us from the love of Christ? Tribulation** or anything else? No, because these things do not break us but delight us *because of him who loved us.** If you have attained wisdom, the *beasts of the earth* are *at*

*Rom 8:35

*Rom 8:37

[6] *Sapientia dicitur a sapore.*

*Job 5:23 *peace with you,** and all that is within you is reconciled
so that your soul no longer serves the flesh but freely
Ps 102:1 blesses God. O welcome and happy bargain to which
the voice of God invites you, saying, *I advise you to buy*
*Rev 3:18 *from me gold tried in the fire:** gold because it buys spiri-
tual things, tried in the fire because it consumes carnal
**affectus* attachments* and worldly desires! *Our God is a consum-*
*Heb 12:29 *ing fire,** the fire of love and the consuming of sin.

7. A precious thing is this wisdom by which we come
to know God and despise the world. Those who find
Prov 3:18 her are blessed indeed if they hold on to her. What
will one give in exchange for her? Spend obedience
and receive wisdom. For this is what Scripture says: *Do*
you desire wisdom? Keep the commandments and the Lord
*Sir 1:33 *will give her to you.** If you wish to be wise, be obedient.
Obedience knows nothing of self-will but submits to
the will of another and is subject to that person's com-
mand. Therefore embrace—yes, embrace—with all the
**affectus* inclination* of your mind and all the exertion of your
body the good of obedience and draw near to the light
of wisdom. Scripture says, *draw near to him and be en-*
*Ps 33:6 *lightened.** Draw near by obedience—there is no safer
or straighter way—and be enlightened by wisdom. For
the one who does not know God *does not know where*
*John 12:35 *he is going,* but *walks in darkness** and *strikes his foot upon*
*Ps 90:12 *a rock.**

Wisdom is light, the true light *which enlightens every*
*John 1:9 *person:** not the person who has a taste for this world
**venientem contra hunc mundum*; see John 1:9 but the person who goes against this world,* and so is
not of the world even though in the world. This is the
‡*novus homo* new person,‡ who has set aside the lazy and depraved
†Col 3:9-10 habits of the old person† and strives *to walk in newness*
*Rom 6:4 *of life,** *knowing there is no condemnation for those who walk*
*Rom 8:1, 4 *not according to the flesh but according to the Spirit.**

impii* It says in Job that in this light *the ungodly *cease from*
*Job 3:17 *turmoil.** The ungodly are those who worship some-
thing other than God, and you worship and appoint to

be your God that thing whose will you strive to do.[7] Well then, so long as you follow your own will you cannot be without inner turmoil, even if you sometimes seem to avoid exterior turmoil. As long as your will is opposed to your reason, you want one thing and are wedded to another.[8] How can you possess peace when you cannot possess yourself? This turmoil of carnal desires, this turmoil of self-will, will not cease in you until your carnal attraction* is transformed and you develop a taste for God. That is why Scripture says that in the light of wisdom *the ungodly cease from turmoil*,* because, *having tasted how sweet the Lord is*,* they cease to be ungodly, from now on worshiping the Creator and not the creature. Once they leave self-will behind, all the restless turmoil slips away.

**carnalis affectus*

*Job 3:17

*Ps 33:9; 1 Pet 2:3

Once the turmoil of affections and the din of thoughts are gone there is peace within you, and God begins to dwell there, for *he makes his place in peace*.* Where God is, there is joy. Where God is, there is serenity. Where God is, there is happiness. Therefore we should desire and seek obedience, for it is through obedience that one obtains the state of wisdom, where there is no sorrow, but where everlasting honor dwells.[9]*

*Ps 75:3

*See Job 10:22

[7] *Impius est quicumque aliud colit quam Deum. Illud enim colis tibique Deum constituis, cuius voluntatem facere niteris.*

[8] *Aliud volente atque aliud vovente*

[9] Bernard here alludes to Job 10:22: *terram miseriae et tenebrarum ubi umbra mortis et nullus ordo et sempiternus horror inhabitans*. By replacing *ordo* with *dolor* and *horror* with *honor*, he neatly inverts its meaning: *ubi nullus dolor, sed sempiternus honor inhabitat.*

Sermon Three

For the Conversion of Saint Paul

1. Today Paul was converted, or, rather, Saul was converted, having turned into Paul. He became like that little child[1] in the gospel of whom the Lord said, *Unless you are converted and become like this little child, you will not enter the kingdom of heaven.**

*Matt 18:3

Perhaps the little child the Lord was speaking of was himself. True, he is *the Lord, great and highly to be praised,** but he is also the *little child* who *has been given to us.** He appears to us now not as great, but little, in order to make himself lovable* and to be a powerful example of the littleness we need to acquire. Your conversion is to a little child so you might learn to be little. When you have been converted, may you become a little child too. Hear how clearly the Lord himself manifests this little child, designated as the model of conversion, pointing out those things that are little in himself as the very things that we should imitate. *Learn from me*, he says, *for I am meek and humble of heart.** Here is a double littleness: humility and meekness. The first is an

*Ps 47:2
*Isa 9:6
**gratum*
*Matt 11:29

[1] *parvulus*, which can be used both as a noun meaning "a little child" or as an adjective describing anything that is "very little." Throughout the sermon Bernard plays on this ambiguity, which is impossible to capture in the English. It is translated here in both ways. The name *Paulus* also means small, and its affinity to the word *parvulus* is part of the word-play as well.

interior littleness, the second an exterior one. Neither one is a little virtue, though, for the one who offers this singular teaching, although he is little, is equally great.

Today Paul was converted. Today he ceased to be Saul. Today he became humble and meek of heart. The confession of his mouth proves the humbling of his heart when he cries out, *Lord, what do you want me to do?** But even more, the very magnitude of the grace he received is proof of it, since grace is only given in exceptional measure to the exceptionally humble. *Acts 9:6

2. Because meekness is, as I have said, an exterior kind of littleness and is therefore more visible [than humility], Paul's conversion proposes meekness to us in three ways, just as there are three battering rams that strike our meekness from without: hurtful words, the loss of things, and bodily injuries. These are the three circumstances where we must exhibit patience* and exercise meekness. Proven virtue* is virtue that none of them seems able to break. *2 Cor 6:4 *Wis 1:3

Consider how at the very moment of his conversion Paul was tested by all three and was found to be truly *Paul*, truly meek and patient in his situation. *Saul, Saul, why do you persecute me? Kicking against the goad is hard on you.** This is a hard word, a reproachful word, a menacing word. With regard to his body, he was struck and thrown to the ground. Was he also tested by loss? Absolutely! The very light of his eyes was taken from him, and, as Scripture says, *when his eyes were opened he could see nothing.** *Acts 26:14 *Acts 9:8

These are the three things that also tested and exercised Job's patience, that man whom God gave us as a renowned example of this virtue. But we leave it to you to pursue this line of thought further. It is enough to counsel you that meekness, to a large extent, is what determines the shape our conversion takes. I say this to the shame of those who are supposed to be already converted but reveal themselves to be inwardly resentful and rebellious[2] when faced with bodily injuries, the loss of things, or—what is even more inexcusable—hurtful words.

[2] *perversos penitus et aversos* instead of *conversos*.

Sermon Four

First Sermon for the Feast of Saint Victor[1]

1. Victor's life and his singular glory challenge all who are upright of heart* to strive not so much for glory as for virtue. To seek for glory before one has practiced virtue and to want a crown without *having competed according to the rules** belong not to an upright heart,* but to a crooked heart. *It is vain for you to rise before the light dawns,** Scripture says. So it is. It is useless for someone to strive for the heights of glory without first having shone with virtue. It is useless for the foolish virgins to rise to meet the bridegroom when their lamps are extinguished. This is precisely why they are foolish: because they glory in empty lamps, having no oil of virtue.*

*Ps 93:15

*2 Tim 2:5

**animi*

*Ps 126:2

*Matt 25:6-8

*Far be it from me to glory except in** the glory of those whom the prophet celebrates when he says, *Lord, they will walk in the light of your face and exult in your name all the day, and in your justice they will be exalted.** Then he adds, *because you are the glory of their virtue.** How beautiful! It is not their glory, but the glory of their virtue

*Gal 6:14

*Ps 88:16-17

*Ps 88:18

[1] *In Natali Sancti Victoris Sermo Primus.* The subject of this sermon is Saint Victor of Arcies, a sixth-century hermit of the Arcis-sur-Aube region of Champagne (France). His relics were moved to the Benedictine monastery of Montiéramey in 837; at the request of the monks of this monastery Bernard wrote the office and two sermons for Victor's feast day (see Bernard, Ep 398).

that he extols. Glory without virtue comes undeservedly, is pursued prematurely, and is seized only at great peril. Virtue is the ladder to glory. Virtue is the mother
*Vulg *gratia* of glory. *False is the glory* and vain is the beauty*‡ not born
‡Prov 31:30 from it. To virtue alone is glory rightfully owed and safely given.

2. Saint Victor lacks neither virtue nor glory. It is worth considering, though, how he came to possess them and in what order. He fought boldly and conquered mightily, and only then was he *crowned with glory*
*Ps 8:6 *and honor.** How could he have remained without glory,
Jer 20:11 this brave warrior, this humble victor?

But he was not without glory even *in the day of* his
*Ps 109:3 *virtue*,* for signs and miracles made him a marvel. Dear
**dilectissimi* friends,* in the life of Victor we have both something worthy of our admiration and something to imitate for our salvation. I marvel that not a vine but a well gave
VSV 4 forth wine in the desert. I marvel and am dumbfounded that an infant still in the womb struck terror in the terrible demons who already knew who he was
VSV 2 and called him by name. Even then his name was not without meaning, because the enemies' flight and the confession wrung from them conceded victory to the tiny baby.

Who does not marvel that a thief possessed by a demon was swiftly delivered from the demon a free man?*
*VSV 5 Who does not derive astonishment from the marvel of a person still wrapped in flesh, who, with the heavens lying open, fixes the eyes of that flesh on the heavenly
Ezek 1:1 light, sees visions of God, is delighted by the angels'
VSV 6–7 singing, and is taught by their oracles? We venerate these things and others like them in the holy man, but we do not strive to imitate them, and for good reason: we can omit them without endangering our salvation, but we cannot undertake them without endangering our salvation. It is safer for us to imitate the things that
**solidiora* are mundane* than those things that are sublime, those things that are more redolent of virtue than of glory.

3. So let us strive to conform to him by our way of life, since, even if we wanted to, we would be unable to model ourselves on his marvels. Let us imitate his sober living and his fervent loving.[2] Let us imitate his gentleness of spirit, his chastity of body, his custody of lips,* and his purity of soul.‡ Let us strive to bridle our anger, to limit our words, to sleep less, to pray more, to *exhort one another with psalms, hymns, and spiritual songs*,* and to join our nights to our days, filling them both with the praise of God.

*Ps 38:2
‡*animi*
*Col 3:16

Let us *strive to imitate the better gifts*.* Let us learn from this man, because he was *meek and humble of heart*.* Let us imitate him, I say, because he stood out as being generous to the poor, cheerful to guests, patient with sinners, and kind to all. This really is better. In these things we have the form that should shape us, while the miracles have the glory that should daze us.[3] Let the latter give us joy and the former build us up. Let his miracles move us and his example improve us.

*1 Cor 12:31
*Matt 11:29

Let us feast, dear friends, for we have been *invited to the rich man's table*,* a table laden with bread and heaped with delights. Is he not a rich man, this man who nourishes us with his examples, protects us with his merits, and gladdens us with miracles? He must be a rich man; today angels and humans are gathered together at his festal banquet! The people come to be nourished and the angels to be delighted. The people come to make progress, and the angels to make merry. What else is a life filled with good things but a table jam-packed with food? Still, not everything is set there for everyone, but so that each person might take what seems personally useful and suitable.

*Prov 23:1-2 LXX

4. As for me, giving thought for my salvation, I will *carefully consider what has been set before me*.* I will be

*Prov 23:1-2 LXX

[2] *sobrium victum devotumque affectum*

[3] *in his forma est cui imprimamur, in miraculis gloria a qua reprimamur*

well warned to pick what is mine and not to touch what belongs to another. I must not stretch out my hand to the glory of miracles, lest by attempting something I have not received from above, I rightfully lose even what I seem to have received. I do not raise my eyes with Victor to pry into heavenly secrets for fear that, *overwhelmed by glory*,* I will recoil in confusion, falling back too late on the counsel of the wise man who said, *Do not seek what is above your reach, and do not probe what is beyond your strength.** The new wine of reddening waters is brought to the table; I do not touch it, because I know it has not been set there for me, for I do not have the same ability to transform elements, to change the natures of things.*

*Prov 25:27

*Sir 3:22

*VSV 4

I also notice at Victor's table the angels he heard singing.* Will these heavenly singers sing for me too? Will those harpists of the Apocalypse *play on their harps* in my presence?* While still living in the body Victor commanded the demons, and after he was freed from the body he freed a man held bound in prison.* These are foods, but they not mine. They are pleasant and tasty dishes, to be sure, but *my soul will not touch them** because I cannot afford, needy as I am, to make a return for such things.

*VSV 7

*Rev 14:2

*VSV 9

*Job 6:7

But if I consider carefully, look, set before my eyes on the saint's table are the rigor of judgment,* the vigor of discipline, the mirror of holiness, the pattern of life, and the mark of virtue. These I pick up without presumption and consume to my good health, and if I pass them over, they will sternly be demanded back.

**censura judicii*

5. Listen now to what I think has really been set on this table for me. If you offer me the *bread of sorrow** and the *wine of compunction** from the rich man's table, I will accept them without qualm, for *I am poor and needy.** *My tears will be my bread by day and by night,* and I will mix my drink with weeping.** This is my portion, since I must grieve for things I have done. I do not think I will

*Ps 126:2
*Ps 59:5
*Ps 85:1
*Ps 41:4
*Ps 101:10

find this food repugnant, however, since *the one who increases knowledge adds to sorrow.*[4]* *Eccl 1:18 LXX

Moreover, if examples of temperance, justice, prudence, or fortitude also appear on the table, I take them without any hesitation, *knowing that I will have to prepare such things myself.** *Prov 23:2 LXX They have been set before me, and I have no doubt that they will be asked of me in return. But will signs and wonders* *Ps 134:9 be demanded from us? Will we need to prepare them for the rich man in return? Brothers, those dishes are there in honor of the one who invited us; they are not the food of the poor.

So you who have been invited, think carefully about what he has placed there for you and what he has placed there for himself. Not absolutely everything that has been set on the table is set there for you. What if a drink is offered to you in a golden cup? You are being served the drink, not the cup. Take the drink and leave the gold. In the same way the head of the family imparts *examples of good works** *Titus 2:7 and uprightness of life to his household in such a way that he reserves the privilege of miracles for himself. In both the one and the other, however, we must glorify the one who gives the gift to live a holy life and to whom the power to perform signs belongs, who lives and reigns in perfect trinity for all ages. Amen.

[4] *Qui apponit scientiam, addidit et dolorem.* A certain amount of sorrow comes with self-knowledge. The connection between self-knowledge and grief is a common theme in Bernard.

Second Sermon for the Feast of Saint Victor[1]

*Phil 4:4
‡*dilectissimi*
†*pietatis*
*Phil 4:4

1. *Rejoice in the Lord,** my friends!‡ Among all the continual favors of his loving-kindness,† he has bestowed on the world a man whose example was to save many. *Again I say, rejoice,** for having been taken from our midst, this man has now drawn near to God to save many more by his intercession.

*Ps 110:4
**pius*
‡i.e., Victor
*Bar 3:38

*The compassionate and merciful Lord** has a man from among the people for whose sake he might pardon the sins of the people. The loving* and merciful advocate‡ has the time and place to make intercession. Yes, he has a place of rest and a time of leisure. *He was seen on the earth** in order to be an example. He was lifted up to heaven in order to be a protector. Here he teaches us how to live; there he invites us to glory. He who was a motivator to action is now a mediator of the kingdom.

*See Rev 3:17
*Ps 40:3
*Ps 22:1-2
*Song 3:11

He is a good mediator, no longer asking anything for himself, but desiring only to impart to us both all the affection of the petitioner and the fruit of the petition. After all, what would he ask for himself when he lacks for nothing?* *The Lord keeps him, gives him life, and makes him blessed in* glory.* *There is nothing* he *shall want in the place of pasture where* he *is given repose.** This is the day of his glorious migration, *the day of his heart's gladness;**

[1] *In Natali Sancti Victoris Sermo Secundus.*

let us rejoice and be glad for him.* He has *entered into the* *Ps 117:24
*power of the Lord;** let us rejoice because now he has *Ps 70:16
more power to save.

2. Today Victor laid aside his body, which seemed to
be the only obstacle to his entering into glory, and
entered, all the more quickly being more unencum-
bered, *into the holy place,* having become like the holy ones* *Heb 9:12
*in glory.** Today the head of the household summons *Sir 45:2
him, and from the last and lowly place that he had
chosen for himself at the Savior's advice, this true friend
goes up higher and *is honored in the presence of those who*
*recline at table with him.** Today, having spurned the *Luke 14:10
world and triumphed over the prince of the world,*
Victor ascends above the world and receives the crown *John 12:31
of victory from the Lord's hand.* *Isa 62:3

He ascends, but with a vast collection of merits, bright
with triumphs, glorious with miracles. The retired sol-
dier takes his rest, and after all the sweat and toil of the
sacred military service he has performed, he is happily
situated, magnificently crowned. *His soul abides in good*
*things.** Where, you ask? *With Abraham and Isaac and* *Ps 24:13
*Jacob in the kingdom of heaven.** With such people and *Matt 8:11
in such a place his soul sits. She sits,* exalted and radi- *i.e., his soul
ant, *filled with joy and praise.** She sits with all her charms, *Isa 35:2
*adorned with her jewels.** She sits surrounded with apples, *Isa 61:10
supported by flowers.* She sits, I tell you, free from *Song 2:5
cares, overflowing with delights,* having ample leisure *Song 8:5
and repose in which to be free for wisdom.

The one who *sat and wept by the rivers of Babylon** *Ps 136:1
now sits at the wellspring of life and dwells* along the **conversatio*
*torrential stream of delight,** whose *flowing waters give joy* *Ps 35:9
*to God's city.** She has discovered for herself *the garden's* *Ps 45:5
*fountain, the well of living waters,** and with the Samaritan *Song 4:15
woman she *drinks the healing water of wisdom,** so that *Sir 15:3
she may *never thirst again.* She is given the fruit of her* *John 4:13
*hands, her works praise her at the gates,** and she glories in *Prov 31:31

*2 Cor 1:12 the *testimony of* her *conscience*,* her own conscience, I say,
1 Cor 10:29 not another's.

She sits among the angels as a worthy companion since she burns with the same desire, shines with the same purity, and is adorned with the same chastity. Victor sits in the midst of the apostles as a man of apostolic grace. He has no reason to hide from the assembly of the prophets, for he glorified and carried
1 Cor 6:20 the one whom they had foretold in his body. Our Victor also feels no need to keep his distance from the victorious choir of martyrs, having offered up *the living*
*Rom 12:1 *sacrifice* of his body* by a difficult daily martyrdom.

3. The veteran soldier sits, now at rest in well-earned sweetness and safety. Yes, he is safe, but he is still concerned for us, for he did not remove his heart of com-
**visceribus pietatis;* Col 3:12 ‡Sir 45:9 passion * when he took off the corruption of the flesh. When *he put on the robe of glory*,‡ he did not clothe himself with forgetfulness of our misery and his mercy.
*Ps 87:13 It is not *the land of oblivion** that Victor's soul inhabits.
Eccl 1:13 It is not the land of toil that occupies him. In fact, it is not a land at all; it is heaven. Does the heavenly habitation harden the souls it receives? Or rob them of their
**pietate* memory? Or strip them of their compassion?*

Brothers, in the spaciousness of heaven hearts do not shrink, they expand. Minds are gladdened, not lost. Affections do not pull back, but reach out farther. In the light of God the memory is clarified, not obscured. In the light of God what is known is not forgotten, but what is not known is learned.

Those celestial spirits who have dwelt in the heavens from the very beginning, do they shun the earth because they are at home in heaven, coming less often to visit and frequent it? Does their ministry of mercy stop
*Matt 18:10 because they are *always looking on the face of the Father*?* No, they are still *all ministering spirits sent to serve those*
*Heb 1:14 *who are laying hold of the inheritance of salvation*.* What then are we to think? Do the angels hasten to and fro

to help human beings while those taken from among
our own ranks have no knowledge of us, or no longer
have any compassion for the things they themselves
suffered? Do those who have never known sorrow feel
ours while *those who came out of the great tribulation** no *Rev 7:14
longer remember what they themselves went through?

I know who said, *the just are waiting for me until you
reward me.** Victor is a just man, and he is surely waiting *Ps 141:8
for us to receive our reward. He is not like Pharaoh's
cupbearer, who kept the good favor he had found for
himself, giving no thought to the man who had been
his fellow prisoner as well as his prophet.* Victor serves *Gen 40:23
Christ and follows Christ.* Christ did not forget his *John 12:26
promise, nor deny fellowship in the kingdom to the
one who shared in his passion.* And the disciple does *2 Cor 1:7
not contradict the teacher.* Victor can *do nothing except* *Matt 10:24
what he sees the teacher *doing. The works which he did,*
Victor *does likewise.** *John 5:19

4. He has entered those heavens that had already lain
open to the gaze of his blessed eyes,* and he now *beholds* *Acts 7:55; VSV 5
*the glory of God with an unveiled face.** He is engrossed, *2 Cor 3:18
but *he does not forget the cry of the poor.** Blessed is this *Ps 9:13
vision by which he is *being transformed into the same image*
*from glory to glory as by the Spirit of the Lord.** *2 Cor 3:18

Small in battle, great in victory, casting out demons
even before he had left his mother's womb,* having *VSV 2
grown in virtues and merits and *living among sinners, he*
*was taken up.** O man of extraordinary holiness, a saint *Wis 4:10
before he was born, a victor in deed before he was
Victor in name! He had already triumphed over the
enemy while still enclosed in the womb.* O holiness *VSV 2
revered by the angels themselves, a holiness from which
the bad angels flee and to which the good angels
throng, with the same fervor but not the same feeling!
It is not easy to say which affirms the holiness of the
man more, the fear of the one or the favor of the other.
While inhabiting the earth with his body and the

heavens with his mind, he heard the voices of heavenly
VSV 7 spirits—sometimes giving him a message as to a friend, and at other times singing magnificent songs of indescribable sweetness.

Victor, truly your soul is one of those jewels that
*VSV *5* appeared to you on the cross.* It was fixed to the cross when it was set in the divine glory and took on the same brilliant image that it found there. He who gave
**expandit gremio* his spirit to the warrior opened his arms* to the victor. O victorious soul, you escaped the world's snares like
Ps 123:7 a sparrow in flight; look now upon our reckless souls, entangled and endangered in those same snares, and rescue us by your protection.

5. O honored veteran, you have exchanged the hard toil of Christian warfare for the repose of angelic bliss! Look upon us, your frail and feeble fellow soldiers, who
Eph 6:12 in the midst of enemy swords and evil spirits are busy praising you. O illustrious Victor, you have gloriously triumphed over both earth and heaven, disdaining the one with a noble pride and seizing the kingdom of the
**pie* other with a tender* violence!‡ *Look down from heaven*†
‡Matt 11:12 on the vanquished of the earth, so that this may be the
†Ps 79:15 culmination of your triumphs—when we perceive that your victory is ultimately ours as well. For if your name has any basis in reality, the full truth of it will be determined by our liberation. That name will surely lack some of its meaning as long as we, who are yours, are not free. How dear, how sweet, how good it is, O Victor, to sing of you, to venerate you, to pray to you *in this*
*Ps 43:20 *place of affliction** and *in this body of death.*‡ *Your name and*
‡Rom 7:24 *your remembrance*† are *honeycomb dripping on the lips* of
†Isa 26:8 captives, *honey and milk under the tongues*° of those who
°Song 4:11 delight in your memory.

Well then, strong athlete, sweet protector, faithful
*Ps 34:2 advocate, *arise to help* us,* so we may rejoice in our rescue and you may glory in a full victory. O Father
*Luke 15:18 Almighty, we *have sinned against you*;* we have become

alien children,* but we have drawn near to you in the person of Victor. As he conquered his worldly desire,* may he also conquer your anger and powerfully restore us to your grace. O Jesus the victor, we praise you in our Victor, knowing that it is you who won the victory in him! Grant him, most merciful Jesus, to glory in the victory he has won in you so that forgetfulness of us does not creep in. Son of God, instill in him the continual remembrance of us in your presence, and inspire him to take up and further our cause at your fearful Judgment, you who live and reign with the Father and the Holy Spirit through all ages, Amen.

*Ps 17:46

**cupiditatem*

Sermon Six

On the Will of God

1. The Lord's will, brothers, first created the angels by bringing them to be and then afterwards blessed them by being brought to be in them. For just as we say that *the Word* that *was in the*
*John 1:1
‡John 1:14
*beginning** *became flesh*‡ when it took on flesh, so the eternal will came to be in the angel[1] when it completely absorbed the angel's will into itself.

What is to prevent us from saying that God's will came to be in the angel when it became the angel's will? This is the angels' ultimate happiness, *the stream of*
*Ps 35:9
heavenly *delight*,* that God's own will has also become the angels' will, so that just as God is pleased by the
*see Heb 1:14
whole of their ministry,* they themselves take delight in everything that they do. Therefore let us pray that just as God's will came to be in the creatures of heaven,
*see Matt 6:10
it may also be done in those on earth,* so that a human being may, like an angel, by *cleaving to God be made one*
*1 Cor 6:17
spirit with him.*

But woe is me! How many obstacles lie in the way, how many things trip me up and hold me back! Malice thrusts itself between our will and God's. So do weak-

[1] Throughout this opening passage Bernard uses the word *facio*. The angels were created when God's will *faciens eosdem*, and then God's will was *in eis facta*. Bernard then compares this action to the incarnation: *sicut Verbum . . . factum caro, sic voluntas illa aeterna in angelo facta est.*

ness, appetite,* and ignorance! There is present in us by nature, or rather by the destruction of our nature, a certain evil inclination* and lust for doing harm, so we find within our wretched souls an unquenchable satisfaction in being mean.* What could be farther from the will of God? Clearly there is *a great abyss fixed between us and** God's will, because God always delights in bestowing favors, while, conversely, a vicious inclination* prompts us, ungrateful as we are, to wish to harm even the innocent. Every *root of bitterness sprouts** from this source. Envy, detractions, and dissensions spring from it, and enmities thrive.

**concupiscentia*

**affectio*

**malitiae delectatio*

*Luke 16:26

**affectio*

*Heb 12:15

We must constantly cut off these poisonous growths with the pruning hook of justice, stripping them away with it, so that we do not do to others what we do not want done to ourselves but, instead, what we wish people to do to us we do to them.* Still, we will never be able to eradicate malice or completely root it from our hearts so long as we are living in this world, which is *wholly set under the Evil One.** Yes, the head of the serpent is being crushed, but, as we often experience, it still lies in wait for our heel.*

*Matt 7:12

*1 John 5:19

*Gen 3:15

2. Second, we are shackled by the weakness of this corruptible body, and this weakness also prevents our will from being able to cleave to God's will. We cannot help but dislike what feels painful to us, and our will is frequently at odds with God's will in these situations. To keep from resisting his will entirely,[2] we need fortitude, the second kind of virtue.

3. Bodily suffering is not the only obstacle, though; our appetites* hold us back too, tugging at us with a whole host of insatiable desires. When can a will so crooked and convoluted ever be united to that will that is perfectly upright and without any deformity? Woe

**concupiscentia*

[2] *ne penitus adversetur. Penitus* can also mean "deeply," with one's innermost being.

is me, Lord my God! Wars rage all around me. On every side are perils and obstacles. Whichever way I turn, I find no safety. I fear both what delights me and what disturbs me. Hunger and refreshment, sleep and vigils, work and rest all take up arms against me. *Give me neither riches nor poverty*, prays the wise man,* because on both sides there is a trap, on both sides danger lies.

*Prov 30:8

If temperance reins in the appetites—indeed it is the only remedy—there will be union, but it will not be full. This is why the apostle confesses, *I consent to the law of God with my mind, but I consent to the law of sin with my flesh.** He partially cleaves to and partially diverges from God's will until that time arrives when *what is perfect comes and what is partial is done away with.**

*Rom 7:16, 25

*1 Cor 13:9-10

4. The fourth obstacle is ignorance, and you are not ignorant of what a large obstacle this is. For how can I promise to follow the guiding will if I do not know it? *I know*, but only *in part*, and not yet *as I am known.** Therefore we must seek with all our desire to grow in prudence, so God may make his will more and more known to us, that we may at all times *know what is acceptable to him.**

*1 Cor 13:12

*Responsory for the 11th Sunday in Ordinary Time; see Wis 9:10

In this way the consummation of the virtues will consummate a union so happy and so desirable that between us and God there will be but one will, and whatever pleases him will also please us. This will be for us—as we said earlier regarding the angels—completely perfect happiness.

5. We also pray that the Lord's kingdom may come,* so we may enjoy absolute security through the authority* of that kingdom. We ask that his name be hallowed‡ because we long even now to rise completely above ourselves into knowledge of him. Indeed when there is happy security and secure happiness for us and in us, we will be rapt by all the ardor of our spirit into the one who is above. *Hallowed be your name.** His name is glory. But when is that glory not holy? Nevertheless,

*Matt 6:10

**potestate*

‡Matt 6:9

*Matt 6:9

we say that his glory is made holy when his name is glorified by our holiness, just as we ask that his will, although it is eternal, be done in us.[3]

And so we ask first for what is greatest: that the unblemished holiness of his glory may become clear to us.[4] Then we request things for ourselves: the establishment of his kingdom's authority for our security and the perfection of his will in us for our joy. But because we do not yet rejoice in this perfection, and are unable to obey God's will without much effort, we need our daily bread.* Plus, as people who often stray from God's will and transgress it, forsaking it,[5] we need to beg for pardon saying, *forgive us our debts*, and the rest.* But in order that we might not fall back into the same transgressions after we have received forgiveness for our sins, we must pray to God to *lead us not into temptation*, but to lead us out of it, and to *deliver us from evil*.* Amen.

*Matt 6:13

*Matt 6:12

*Matt 6:13

[3] *Fieri tamen dicitur sancta gloria eius, cum in sanctitate glorificatur a nobis, sicut et voluntatem eius, qui aeterna est, in nobis fieri postulamus.*

[4] *ut nobis gloriae illius innotescat sanctitas illibata.*

[5] *saepius quoque aberrantes ab ea et delinquentes, hoc est derelinquentes eam. . . .*

Sermon Seven

On the Mercies of the Lord

*Ps 88:2 **1.** *I will sing forever of the mercies of the Lord.** Why is
it that a foolish little thought murmurs to me
about what a burden this penance is, making
it weigh heavily upon my neck? There is another bur-
Matt 11:30 den I feel, one that is undeniably sweeter, but also far
greater. For God so burdens me with his mercies, so
encompasses me, so overwhelms me with his kind-
nesses, that I am unable to feel any other burden. *What*
*Ps 115:12 *shall I repay the Lord for all he has given to me*?*

He has given me so much, has given me back so
much, and you speak to me of some other burden? *My*
*Ps 76:4 *spirit faints**—yes, faints—at the thought of all his many
kindnesses. And even though I am incapable of properly
thanking him, my soul absolutely abhors ingratitude.
**peremptoria res* Ingratitude is a deadly thing,* an enemy of grace, a foe
of salvation. I tell you that it seems to me that nothing
so displeases God, especially in children of grace, in
people of conversion, as ingratitude. It blocks the paths
of grace, and where there is ingratitude, grace no longer
finds an entrance; it has no room.

And so, brothers, I have *great sorrow and continual an-*
*Rom 9:2 *guish in my heart,** seeing some so prone to levity, so
quick to laugh and say silly things. I am greatly alarmed,
fearing that perhaps they are being too forgetful of
God's mercies and too ungrateful for all his many favors,
and that grace will one day forsake them, that grace
which they do not reverence as grace.

2. What shall I say about those stubborn souls who remain hardened in murmuring and impatience? Or what about those who regret having ever clung to God* and, contrary to custom and even contrary to reason, follow up a good deed by repenting for it? Such people are not only ungrateful for God's mercies but even offer insult in return for them. Those who serve him in sadness and rancor dishonor—to the extent they can—the one who has called them, if they are even capable of serving him in that sadness that is according to the flesh and produces death.* Do you think that they will be given more grace? Or does it not seem more likely that *even what they* seem to *possess will be taken away from them*?* Are gifts given to the ungrateful not considered squandered? Does the giver not regret having ever given the gift that seems lost?

*1 Cor 6:17

*2 Cor 7:10

*Matt 13:12; 25:29

People who desire not only to keep the gifts of grace they have received but to multiply them should be grateful and devout. There are none who do not, if *they seek*, easily *find** reasons that they are much indebted to God, since *there is no one who can hide from his heat.** But we in particular, whom God has set apart for himself and taken to serve him alone, should—if, as the apostle says, *we have not received the spirit of this world but the spirit which is from God, so that we may know what God has given us**—find countless reasons for offering him unceasing thanks. Who among us cannot confess, *Your mercy towards me is great*?* And so, out of the great number of the Lord's mercies I wish briefly to point some out to you, so that *the one who is wise may have the opportunity to become wiser.**

*Matt 7:8

*Ps 18:7

*1 Cor 2:12

*Ps 85:13

*Prov 9:9

3. I see in myself seven mercies of the Lord that I believe you will also easily discover within yourselves. The first is that he guarded me from many sins while I was still in the world. (I am not saying that this is the first of all the mercies God has lavished on me, but that it is the first of the seven I will speak about.) Who does not see that just as I have fallen into many sins, I might have fallen into still many more had the loving-kindness* of the Almighty not spared me? I confess and will confess: *Unless the Lord had helped me my soul would soon have fallen into every sin.** How great is the favor of his loving-kindness! He upheld me by his grace, ungrateful and unappreciative though I was. In his great kindness, he protected me from additional sins, defiant and disdainful though I was.

**pietas*

*Ps 93:17

And your second mercy towards me, Lord, how can words express* how kind, how generous, how gracious it was? I was sinning, and you pretended not to notice.[1] I did not refrain from committing heinous acts, and yet you held back the lash. For a long time *I persevered in my wickedness,** and you, Lord, persevered in your mercy. But what good would this waiting have been if my repentance had not followed? Condemnation would have piled up while the Lord said, *you did these things, and I was silent.**

*Eccl 1:8

*Ps 128:3

*Ps 49:21

4. And so there was a third mercy: God visited my heart and changed it so that those things that had wrongly seemed sweet to me before became bitter. I *who used to enjoy doing evil and revelled in wicked things** began at last to *reflect on my years* before him *in the bitterness of my soul.** At that time, Lord, *you shook the land* of my heart *and disturbed it; heal its distress, for it has been shaken.** For many have been *led by repentance,** but it was fruitless because their repentance was condemned just as their earlier fault had been.[2] And so this was the fourth mercy, that you received the penitent with

*Prov 2:14

*Isa 38:15

*Ps 59:4

*Matt 27:3

[1] *Ego peccabam et tu dissimulabas.*

[2] The allusion is to Matthew 27:3, which tells how Judas, "led by repentance," tried to return the thirty pieces of silver to the chief priests. It is not enough to be repentant, Bernard says: the repentance must be met with forgiveness. While the priests did not receive Judas with mercy, God received the penitent with mercy.

mercy and let me be counted among those of whom the psalmist says, *blessed are they whose sins have been remitted.** *Ps 31:1

5. Next is the fifth mercy, by which you provided me with the strength to practice self-restraint from now on and to live a more blameless life, lest I suffer a relapse and my last fault be worse than the first.* It is absolutely clear that it is your power alone, Lord God, not human power, that removes the yoke of sin from our necks once we have put it on, because everyone who commits sin is a slave of sin* and cannot be freed except by a strong hand.* But now, after you have delivered me from evil* by these five mercies, you give me good things with the remaining two in order that what is written may be done: *Turn aside from evil and do good.** These two mercies are the grace to acquire merits—in other words, you give me the ability to live a good life*—and the hope of laying hold of what is to come—allowing an unworthy and sinful person to learn from numerous experiences of your goodness to dare to hope even for the things of heaven.

*see Matt 27:64

*John 8:34

*Exod 13:3

*Matt 6:13

*Pss 33:15; 36:27

**bonae conversationis*

Sermon Eight

On the Seven Gifts of the Holy Spirit

1. *The mediator between God and humanity, the man Christ Jesus,** chose to use the seven gifts of the Holy Spirit to reconcile the human race. Let us reflect, as best we can, on why this was fitting and necessary.[1]

*1 Tim 2:5

Because he was coming to be the mediator between two discordant parties, he had to align himself with them both. He needed to be subject to God the Father in faithful reverence by the spirit of fear* and to descend to be with fallen humanity in merciful compassion by the spirit of piety.[2]* For unless he had joined himself* to the former through fear and the latter through pity,* neither would have entrusted their cause to him, and he would neither have conciliated God to humanity nor reconciled humanity to God.

*Isa 11:3

*Isa 11:2

**conveniret*

**pietatem*

[1] *qua convenientia et necessitate.* Throughout the sermon Bernard returns to these two words, though not in any systematic way. Because *convenientia* has different meanings depending on the context, I have translated it differently in different cases while providing a Latin gloss.

[2] The Latin word *pietas* has a broader meaning than the English word *piety*, expressing faithful and devoted love, and sometimes with a meaning synonymous to mercy. Because the gift of the Spirit is usually identified as *piety*, I have used that word here, but as Bernard is using it in its sense of loving mercy, I have elsewhere translated *pietas* differently.

Moreover, in order to know what he owed to each party, and in what measure, he needed to have the spirit of knowledge.* For it was not partners or equals who engaged in this dispute, but the matter was between a lord and his servant, the Creator and the creature. Therefore he had to take into consideration the salvation of the servant in such a way that he in no way deviated from the obedience due the Lord. After all, a greater tie of obligation held him to God, since he was bound to humanity by merely one chain, that of compassion,* while two chains, fear and love,* bound him to God. This is why when he was brought to the point of needing to choose between disregarding[3]* God's will and offending the synagogue—to which, by his own confession, he had been especially sent*—he allowed the synagogue to be scandalized and himself to be crucified by acting in obedience to the Father. In fact the whole spirit of knowledge decreed it.[4]

*Isa 11:2

**pietatis*

**timore et amore*

**postponere*

*Matt 15:24

The first human being, when he was in a similar situation, paid no attention to following and heeding this spirit of knowledge and rashly sank into evil as a result. If only he had clung fast to God with fear and love as he rightly should have, when God forbade him to take from the tree of good and evil,* a disordered devotion* would never have led him to wrongly consent to the woman's coaxing him to transgress.*

*Gen 2:17

**pietate*

*Gen 3:6

Yet because that *strong well-armed man*,* the devil, held humanity bound, whom Christ had come to liberate,

*Luke 11:21

[3] The Latin—*Unde et cum ad hoc ventum est ut, aut voluntatem Dei praeponere, aut synagogam . . . offendere oportere, synagogam potius scandalizari et se crucifigi oboediendo Patri permisit*—does not make sense. It seems possible that an error early in the manuscript tradition substituted *praeponere* for *postponere*. I am here reading *praeponere* as *postponere*. (I am grateful to Stefano Mula for his assistance with this passage.)

[4] *quod quidem totum spiritum scientiae procuratum est.* The grammar of this line is irregular.

Christ needed fortitude to overthrow the strong man
and free the captive. He did indeed have this fortitude,
*Ps 23:8 of which the psalmist sang, *the Lord is strong and mighty*,*
*Ps 92:1 and again, *the Lord clothed himself with strength*.* Yes, with
this strength he strongly waged war against the powers
Eph 2:2 of the air and powerfully plundered hell.

For this endeavor he needed a wonderful and lofty
counsel if he was to overcome the ancient enemy when
they met in battle and to offer a sufficient sacrificial
victim for the sin of humanity, which was unable to
appease God on its own. But what did he offer to God
the Father? Being in the form of God, he was equal to
Phil 2:6 God, and in his divine nature he possessed nothing
other than what the Father had. After all, since *all that*
*John 16:15 *the Father has is* his,* it follows that what he has by
nature, insofar as it is divine, the Father has as well. It
is for this reason he says, *all that the Father has is mine*,*
*John 16:15 and again, *the Father and I are one*.* Therefore, since he
*John 10:30 needed to have something to offer, and, as we just
briefly explained, it could not come from his divinity,
nothing remained except for him to sacrifice the
human nature, pure from every stain of sin, that he had
taken from a virgin's flesh, in order to *abolish the sentence*
*Col 2:14 *that stood against us** for sin and reconcile humanity with
God.

But if he did this by dying, how did he conquer the strong man? Who wins by dying? And yet, if he did not conquer the strong man, how did he rescue the prisoner? On the other hand, if he overcame the enemy while alive, as other combatants do, what sacrificial victim did he offer for the sin of humanity? And if he did not offer a sacrificial victim, how did he reconcile humanity to God?

2. And so by the spirit of counsel a marvelous plan was devised: that by a new and unheard of kind of combat, life would contend with death and in dying would overcome death. In this way both sides were taken care of. On the one hand, the devil, having unjustly attacked the one who was free from all sin with the punishment for sin, would be justly condemned, while on the other hand, the pitiable wretch in need of a cure would by that same sacrifice be mercifully reconciled to God by the blood of the Mediator. No one should think this is in any way incompatible with* or opposed to fortitude. It showed more strength and power for a dead man to rise from the grave than for a living man to come down from the cross.* And we should note that because he is coeternal with the Father according to his divinity and equal to him in all things, he himself had no need for this sacrifice. Because he was God, the kingdom of God was never not his. Instead, he was thinking of* his brothers. He, the firstborn brother,* possessing an intrinsic right to reign and purchasing another by the price of his sacrifice, was looking out for his brothers with a marvelous and indescribable love.

**inconveniens*

*Matt 27:42

**consuluit*

*Rom 8:29

Subject to the Father by the spirit of fear, he descended to join humanity by the spirit of piety. He discerned what he owed to each one by the spirit of knowledge, and by the spirit of fortitude he triumphed over the enemy. By the spirit of counsel he chose this most mighty mode of victory.

3. We have said something about each of these five gifts, but it remains for us to try to say a little something about the two that are left, wisdom and understanding*—at least inasmuch as God provides us with something to say. In order to make what we say easier to understand, however, it might be helpful to draw from what is visible some fitting likeness to these things that are invisible.

*Isa 11:2

4. Think of someone who is wasting away and so debilitated that every lower part of his body is dead before it is dead, so only his head is alive, and he lives with only three senses: vision, hearing, and smell. Does it not seem to you that the soul that resides in such a body is sort of constricted—as far as giving life and sentience are concerned, I mean—exercising its powers* only in these three senses, having abandoned the rest? As long as this person lacks the sense of taste, no food can benefit him. You can put as much good food into him as you like, and it will not help him so much as weigh him down.

**vires*

But if the soul reaches out, so to speak, reviving those lower parts for just a moment, and the one who was so desperately sick begins to taste a little something, the person's friends immediately exult. Hope of life and health return to the invalid. Afterwards, as this taste encourages the appetite more fully and passes along the good juices* of good food through the stomach to the lower members, and after he who was called sick has spent some more time eating and with greater enjoyment, it often happens that his health completely returns. See all the good things the soul provided to this body from a taste! If it had not, surely even the upper part of the body would have grown weak.

**humores*

5. Let us now return to the starting point of this scenario and see, with the Lord's help, how these things correspond* to the mystery of our restoration point by point. I understand the human body here to represent every rational creature, and the living soul, which has life on its own and gives life to everything else, to represent *the power and wisdom of God.** When the world was languishing under sin and the punishment for sin, and what God had made had been deserted by life and, being without life, so to speak, was already dead,[5] the power and wisdom of God was active only in the angels, the patriarchs, and the prophets, as though in the three senses of the head: sight, hearing, and smell.

**conveniant*

*1 Cor 1:24

[5] *Quae utique mundo peccato et peccati poena languido et ab eo quidem factus est vita deserto et quasi absente vita praemortuo.*

Though the rest of creation had been abandoned, God's power and wisdom did not withdraw the benefits of its knowledge from them.

There is nothing wrong with saying that eyes symbolize the angels, ears the patriarchs, and nostrils the prophets. The eyes are a part of the body in which they were created, and yet, because of their keen perception and their luminous clarity, they surpass all the other parts of the body by their immense dignity. The same is true of the angels; although one can rightly say that they are a part of rational creation because they were created, nevertheless, because of their keen knowledge and understanding and their spiritual nature, they surpass all the other creatures by an unparalleled privilege.

The ears, for their part, represent the patriarchs who listened obediently to God when he asked them to do great things. The nostrils we can interpret to be the prophets, who by divine inspiration breathed in like a fragrance the knowledge of the Christ who was to come long after them. Their figure and herald is that peerless patriarch—in this case a prophet—who exhaled to others the fragrance that he had first breathed in, saying, *behold, the fragrance of my son is like the fragrance of a fertile field that God has blessed.** *Gen 27:27

So that this body's lower, dead, parts—the sinful, dead, people—could be made alive, could be justified, that is, the soul needed to descend beneath the head to the throat and transmit new life to the body through the taste. In other words, it was necessary that the Wisdom of God *when it was in the form of God emptied himself and took the form of a slave,** conferring life—justice—to *Phil 2:6-7
the human race by *faith working through love,** for *without* *Gal 5:6
*faith it is impossible to please God.** *Heb 11:6

We should note that the gift of wisdom neatly corresponds* to the sense of taste because flavor resides in ***convenit*
the taste, and the word *flavor** seems to have been taken ***sapor*
from the word for being wise.* It is well said that flavor ***sapio*

resides in the taste, because *in Christ are hidden all treasures of wisdom and knowledge.** *Col 2:2-3

But because we pointed out that the sense of taste is situated lower than the head, lower than the head's other three senses, that is, the question might arise: how can we regard Christ to be lower than these orders?[6] The psalmist testifies, however, that Christ was made to be lower than the angels,* saying, *you made him a little lower than the angels.** With regard to the patriarchs and prophets, we say that Christ was in some way less than they not by nature but by grace, not in terms of the privilege of his dignity but as to the exercise of his power. After all, we read that Abraham conquered five kings* and that Elijah slew fifty kings and fifty of the kings' soldiers with fire summoned from heaven,* and throughout the Scriptures we find many stories like this about other Old Testament fathers. About Christ we read no such thing, even though the gospel reminds us that he could have certainly done much greater things than these.* Instead, as it is written, *a shaken reed he did not break and a smoldering wick he did not quench,** and *like a sheep led to the slaughter and as a lamb before its shearer he did not open his mouth.**

*Heb 2:7 *Ps 8:6; Heb 11:6 *Gen 14:15 *2 Kgs 1:10-14 *see John 5:19-20 *Matt 12:20 *Isa 53:7

See what the Wisdom of God bore in a human being, how lowly and arduous! See what the Wisdom of God mercifully conferred upon his members, how lofty and sweet! There is no doubt that if Wisdom had not done this, even the upper members would have continued to lack something. The lives of the patriarchs and prophets would have been fruitless. The number of the angels themselves, which shrank when the apostate spirits fell, would never have been restored once the tenth drachma had been found.[7]* *see Luke 15:8-9

[6] i.e. the angels, patriarchs, and prophets.

[7] The idea that redeemed humanity will fill up the places left by the fallen angels has a long history in patristic thought as far back

Now though, this Mediator abundantly pours forth the dew of spiritual graces upon *the Church, which is his body*,* and enkindles its desire through love. And so it makes daily progress towards salvation until, the whole body having attained perfect health,* *we all arrive at perfect manhood in the measure of the full stature of Christ*.*

*Eph 1:22-23

**salutem*

*Eph 4:13

6. As for understanding, since we promised to speak about it, I would like just briefly to consider how it resides in the taste. Along with that flavor that enables everyone to judge or discern whether a thing is sweet or bitter, a doctor or skilled physician's sense of taste also possesses understanding. When they take a sip of something, they understand by tasting it how hot or cold, dry or wet it is.[8] In the same way Wisdom, in which God the Father arranged all things from all eternity, understands everything in a way that is real and yet incomprehensible to us. By means of understanding, Wisdom discerns not only between day and night, but between day and day,* and enables those who belong to her to discern the gifts of understanding. Through the same Jesus Christ our Lord.

*Rom 14:5

---

as Augustine. Bernard mentions it a number of times. See in particular SC 62.1, SC 77.4, and SC 78.1. The idea that the ten drachmas of Luke 15:8-10 symbolize the nine choirs of angels plus the tenth, the order of humanity, appears in Gregory the Great's *Homiliae in Evangelia* 2.34.

[8] These four qualities were believed to be related to the four bodily humors. Much of medieval medicine depended on giving the patient preparations that would balance the body's humors by introducing the opposite qualities. These qualities are separate from temperature and moisture, which are easily discerned and presumably don't require advanced knowledge or understanding.

Sermon Nine

On Saint Malachy

*dilectissimi

*2 Cor 5:6; peregrinamur

*Rom 12:15

*Ps 67:4

*Sir 50:1; 44:16-17; Antiphon for Lauds of a bishop confessor

‡Luke 1:75

†1 Cor 9:18; MalV 43

°Eph 6:17

*Matt 11:30

*Isa 49:6

*Ps 2:8

*see Matt 27:6-7; 1 Pet 1:19

1. My friends,* it is obvious that *while we are being held by the body we are away from the Lord.** This pitiable exile as well as the awareness of our sins calls for our grief rather than our joy, but nevertheless, since the apostle's lips urge us to *rejoice with those who rejoice*,* the day and its occasion demand that we rise up in all gladness. For if, as the prophet believed, *the just exult in the presence of God*,* Malachy surely exults, he *who in his days pleased God and was found to be a just man.** *In holiness and justice he* ministered *in God's presence.*‡ God was pleased with the ministry and pleased with the minister.

Why wouldn't Malachy be pleasing to God? He *offered the gospel without cost*† and spread it throughout his country. He tamed the savage barbarism of his people, the Irish. By *the sword of the Spirit*,° he placed foreign nations under the light yoke of Christ,* restoring the Lord's inheritance to him unto the ends of the earth.*

O fruitful ministry! O faithful minister! Is it not through Malachy that the Father fulfilled his promise to the Son? Is this not the man the Father had in mind when he said to the Son, *I will give you the nations for your inheritance and the ends of the earth for your possession?** How gladly the Savior received what he himself had bought, bought with the price of his blood,* the shame of the cross, and the horror of the passion! How gladly he received it from the hands of Malachy because

Malachy freely offered his ministry! He welcomed the minister's free offering* and was pleased with the ministry's success at converting sinners. Welcome and pleasing is simplicity of eye* in the minister. Welcome and pleasing is the salvation of the people by his ministry.

**gratum munus gratuitum*
*Matt 6:22

2. Even if Malachy's ministry had been less effective, the Lord would still have looked with approval on him and his works. Purity is the Lord's friend, simplicity his companion, and it is part of his justice to value a work by its intention and to judge the condition of the whole body by the soundness of the eye.* But as it is, *great are the works of the Lord, wonderfully wrought through all the desires* and efforts of Malachy.* Great, plentiful, and mightily good are these works, but all the better for having the good start of a pure intention.

*Matt 6:22
*Ps 110:2

What work of mercy* escaped Malachy? He was poor with himself but rich to the poor. He stood out as a father of orphans, husband of widows, and defender of the oppressed.* He was a *cheerful giver*,‡ who asked for things rarely and received them with reticence. He worked hard and with much success at reestablishing peace between those at odds with each other. Who was as merciful in showing compassion, as prompt in giving assistance, and as frank in giving correction as he was?*

**pietatis*
*Ps 67:6
‡2 Cor 9:7
*MalV 42

He was zealous, but without lacking knowledge,* the moderator of zeal. Yes, he was *weak with the weak*,* but he was no less strong with the strong: opposing the proud, lashing out at tyrants, acting as instructor* to kings and princes. It was he who by his prayers deprived a king of his sight when he did evil and restored it to him once he was humbled.* It was he who handed over those who broke the peace he had forged to the spirit of error,* thwarting the evil they had planned to do and forcing them to make peace again, baffled and befuddled as they were by what had befallen them.* It was to him that a river dutifully offered its assistance in opposing other violators of this same pact, wonder-

*see Rom 10:2
*1 Cor 9:22
**magister*; MalV 9
*MalV 60
*1 John 4:6
*MalV 58

fully frustrating the efforts of the godless by its interference. There were no showers, no floods, no gathering clouds, no melting snow, when suddenly what had been a small rivulet became a mighty stream. The swelling river rushed and rose, not allowing a single one of those
MalV 59 intending to do evil to cross over.

*Ps 77:3 **3.** *How great are the things we have heard and known** about this man's zeal and the vengeance he took on enemies, and yet at the same time he was *sweet and gentle
*Ps 85:5 *and full of mercy to all** who were in need. He lived for all as if he were the sole parent of all, and like a hen
Matt 23:37 warming and protecting her chicks he cherished and
*Ps 60:5 protected everyone *in the shelter of his wings.** He did not discriminate according to sex, age, rank, or social standing. No one was without a place in the wide-open
**pietatis* bosom of his mercy.* Whatever the trouble, when
Jonah 2:3; Introit 2nd Thursday of Lent, Collect for the Dedication of a Church someone cried out to him he considered the trouble to be his own, the only difference being that he patiently tolerated his own troubles, while those of others, which he bore with compassion, he usually found intolerable.[1]

Sometimes, filled with zeal, he felt moved to confront people on the behalf of others, so that by rescuing the
see Ps 34:10 needy and restraining the strong he might show concern for the salvation of all. And so he got angry, but only to avoid the sin of not getting angry; for as the
*Ps 4:5 psalm says, *Be angry and do not sin.** Anger did not rule
*Prov 16:32; *animo* him, but he himself ruled his heart.* He was his own master, and having conquered himself, he could not be overcome by anger. He held it in his hand. It came when he called and left without erupting. It acted only with his consent and not out of compulsion. He made use of it without being consumed by it.[2] And he exercised that same rigorous discipline and extreme caution

[1] *in sua patiens, in aliena compatiens erat, plerumque et impatiens.*

[2] *Nutu non impetu ferebatur. Non urebatur illa, sed utebatur.*

in controlling and restraining all the other movements of his inner and outer man.

For he was not so focused on everyone else that the one person he left unprotected was himself or that he excused himself alone from his general concern. He worried over himself. He guarded himself. The result was that ultimately he belonged wholly to himself and wholly to others, so that charity never seemed to hinder or hamper him from keeping guard over himself, or self-concern from serving the common good. If you saw the man immersed in the crowds and enveloped by cares, you would declare that he had been born for his people and not himself. If you saw the man in solitude, dwelling with himself,[3] you would think that he lived only for God and himself.

4. He remained in the crowds without being troubled, and the time he gave to leisure he spent without being idle.[4] How could he be idle when he *was practicing the precepts of* the Lord?* Even if he had time free from people's needs, it was not a holiday from holy meditations, fervent prayer, or the leisure of contemplation itself. *Ps 118:23

At such times of leisure he spoke seriously or not at all. His expression was either filled with attentive courtesy or else cast down and self-contained. What the wise consider to be no little praise can be said of him: *his eyes were in his head*,* never wandering except when virtue demanded it. His smile[5] always indicated or *Eccl 2:14

[3] *secum habitantem*. Bernard also uses this phrase in Div 31.1 regarding the soul that is able to guard itself from idle thoughts. Gregory the Great uses the same expression in his *Dialogues* to describe Saint Benedict (2.3). The prodigal son "returned to himself," *in se reversus*, Gregory explains, but the saint never left himself, *habitavit secum*. See Gaetano Raciti's note in SCh 526:270.

[4] *Sine turbatione versabatur in turbis. Sine otio tempus, quod otio dederat, transigebat.*

[5] *Risus*. This word can refer either to a smile or to laughter.

elicited love, and was itself rare. On those occasions when he brought it out (for it never broke out) it declared the happiness of his heart in such a way that it did not diminish the charm of his face but increased it. It was so modest that it could not be suspected of frivolity, and although it was a little smile, it was still enough to free his cheerful face from every mark or cloud of sadness.*

*MalV 43

*Ps 19:4

*2 Cor 2:15

O perfect gift! O rich holocaust!* O faithful service offered with mind and hand! How good was the fragrance offered to God* by the prayers of his leisure! How good was the fragrance offered to the people by the sweat of his labor!

*Sir 45:1

*MalV 12; MalH stanza 2.3

5. Because of these things Malachy *was loved by God and the people** and deserved to be welcomed into the company of the angels on this day, having become in reality what he was called by name.[6]* He was already an angel, as pure as the name he bore, but now the meaning of that glorious name is more happily perfected in him, for now he rejoices in a glory and a happiness equal to that of the angels.

*MalH stanza 3

*Dan 5:13

*Ps 117:24

Let us also rejoice, dear friends, that our angel has ascended to his fellow citizens* and now acts as an ambassador for the children of captivity,* reconciling us to the hearts of the blessed and making known to them the petitions of the wretched. *Let us rejoice and exult,** I say, because that heavenly court now contains one of our own, one who cares for us and shields us with his merits, having already taught us by his example and strengthened us by his miracles.

*from the prayer *in spiritu humiliatis* at the offertory of the Mass; Dan 3:39

‡Ps 42:4

6. This holy bishop, who so often brought peace offerings to heaven *in a spirit of humility*,* has today himself *entered in to the altar of God*‡ as both offering and priest. The sacrificial rite has now been transformed

[6] The name *Malachy* means *my angel* in Hebrew.

into something better for this departed priest; the font
of tears has dried up, and every holocaust offering is
now seasoned* *with gladness and exultation.*‡ *Lev 2:13 ‡Ps 44:16

Blessed be the Lord, Malachy's *God*, who *has visited his
people** through the ministry of such a bishop and who, *Luke 1:68
now that Malachy has been taken up into the holy city,* *see Matt 4:5
does not cease to console us in our captivity with the
memory of such sweetness. May Malachy's spirit *exult
in the Lord,** since now, relieved of the weight of physical *Luke 1:47
substance,* he is no longer hampered by mucky earthy *MalH stanza 1
matter from passing with all swiftness and exuberance
beyond all creatures, corporeal and incorporeal, and
pressing on with his whole being into God,[7] and cleav-
ing to him, being one spirit with him* for all eternity. *1 Cor 6:17

7. *Holiness is fitting to* this *house,** where the memory *Ps 92:5
of such great holiness is celebrated.* Saint Malachy, *MalT 2
serve this house *in holiness and justice.** Have mercy on *Luke 1:75
us who in the midst of so much misery *belch forth** *the *eructamus
memory of your abundant sweetness.** Great was the gift *Ps 144:7
of God's loving-kindness* that made you seem little in *pietatis
your own eyes and great in the eyes of him who did
great things through you by saving your country, and
great things for you * by admitting you into his glory. *Luke 1:49

Your feast, dedicated to honoring your virtues, furthers our own salvation by your merits and prayers. *The
glory of your holiness,** which we celebrate with a festival *Ps 144:5
that the angels continue to prolong, will be a just cause of joy for us so long as it also bears fruit within us. As you leave us, may we who gather together today at your banquet of delights be allowed to keep some remnants of the Spirit's fruits with which you are so laden in your ascent.

[7] *pergat totus in deum.* This expression appears seven times in Bernard's published works: Dil 27 and 39, Div 8.9 and 10.3, Ep 11.8, and OS 3.2. He also seems to play on it in SC 46.6. See SCh 526:274.

*Deut 34:9; 2 Kgs 2:9, 15
‡Luke 1:17
†Sir 45:6
*MalT 4; MalV 75

8. Be for us, we beg, another Moses, or another Elijah, and give us a share of your spirit,* for you came *in the spirit and power*‡ of them both. Your life, O Malachy, is *the law of life and discipline*;† your death, the port of death and the portal to life.[8]* Your memory is a taste of sweetness and grace. Your presence *is the crown of glory in the hand of the Lord your God.**

*Isa 62:3
*Ps 51:10
*Ps 44:8

O *fruitful olive tree in the house of God!** O *oil of gladness** that anoints and illumines, soothing with kind deeds and shining with miracles, make us sharers in the light and sweetness which you now enjoy! O sweet scented lily, budding and blossoming eternally before the Lord and spreading everywhere the life-giving scent of sweetness,* you *whose memory is a blessing*‡ to us below and whose presence is an honor to those above, grant that those who sing your praises may not be cheated of a share of such fullness!

*Eph 5:2
‡Sir 45:1

O *great light,** *light shining in the darkness,*‡ whose miracles and merits are rays that brighten this prison below and *gladden that city* on high,* chase the darkness of vice from our hearts with the bright splendor of virtue! O *morning star,** brighter than all the rest because you are nearer to the day and more like the sun, deign to go before us so that we may walk in the light* as children of light and not children of darkness!* O dawn glinting upon the earth, but also noon-day radiance flooding the heights of heaven, receive us into the fellowship of that light that illumines you, that causes you to blaze out far and wide and to glow sweetly within as you stand before our Lord Jesus Christ, who reigns with the Father and the Holy Spirit, God, through all ages.

*Gen 1:16
‡John 1:5
*Ps 45:5
*Rev 22:16
*Ps 88:16
*Eph 5:8; 1 Thess 5:5

[8] *mors tua, mortis portus et porta vitae.*

SERMON TEN

For the Feast of Saint Benedict

1. On the Gospel Reading: *Simon Peter said to Jesus** *Matt 19:27; gospel for the liturgy

1. *Simon Peter said to Jesus, "See, we have left all things and followed you."*‡ Brothers, I believe that the words of this reading are the very words that the church is referring to when she sings in the psalmody, *Because of the words of your lips I have kept to hard ways.** These are the words that move people to take up voluntary poverty and contempt for the world. These are the words that gave birth to monasteries, that filled the cloisters with monks and the woods with laybrothers.*

‡Matt 19:27

*Ps 16:4

**conversis*

*Simon Peter said to Jesus.** Simon talks to Jesus familiarly and converses with him as with a friend. Obedience is indeed kin and neighbor to salvation[1] as long as it does not waver or falter but is *founded upon solid rock.**

*Matt 19:27

*Matt 7:24-25

*See, we have left all things and followed you.** Well done! *He exulted like a giant to run the course,** and you would have been unable to follow after this runner if you had been weighed down with burdens. You are right, I say, to have left all things in order to follow the one *who is over all,** because *our sufficiency is from* him,‡ and *God will be all in all.*†

*Matt 19:27

*Ps 18:6

*Rom 9:5

‡2 Cor 3:5

†1 Cor 15:28

[1] The name Simon means "listener" and was by extension interpreted as "obedience" by Jerome (*Interpretatio* 103 [PL 23:849]). The name Jesus means "salvation" (*Interpretatio* 114 [PL 23:855]).

*Matt 19:27 **2.** *See,* he says, *we have left all things,** not only the
riches of the world but also the cravings of the soul.
After all, those who hold on to themselves have not
left all things. On the contrary, those who have not left
themselves gain nothing by having left everything else,
since no other burden weighs more heavily on one
than one's own self. For what lord is so wicked, what
tyrant so cruel, that he would not spare his slave boy
more than the self-will spares the self? Under self-will's
dominion there is no rest, never a break. The more it
knows you are weary of obeying it, the more it drives
you, the more it badgers you, the more it adds to your
load, pitiless and merciless as a cruel mistress. *O guardian
of humanity, why have you set me against you and made me*
*Job 7:20 *a burden to myself?** Woe is me! I have cast off the light
Matt 11:30 yoke and sweet burden and purchased for myself the
five yokes of the bodily senses, surrendering myself to
unyielding compulsion and miserable servitude. Happy
are they who, hearing the divine call crying out in
mercy, *Come to me all you who labor and are heavily bur-*
*Matt 11:28 *dened,** respond with heart and deed, *Lord, we have left*
*Matt 19:27 *all things and followed you.**

Observe how in the past, before the Word became
John 1:14 flesh and lived among us, the Fathers of ancient times
followed God by cleaving to the one Spirit with the
1 Cor 6:17 spirit alone. But now, after the incarnation, God must
be followed with the body as well. We read, therefore,
that these aforementioned Fathers, although they were
great and righteous men, abounded in earthly riches.
From now on, however, unless one renounces all that
Luke 14:33 one has, one cannot be the disciple of him who *al-*
*2 Cor 8:9 *though he was rich became poor for our sakes.**

*Matt 19:27 **3.** Next it says, *then what will we have?** You have
already left all things, you already follow him alone and
have followed him for a long time, and this is the first
time you are asking what you will receive? You really
Ps 17:45 are Simon; you really obey as your ear hears and not
as agreed to by contract. But now I beg you, Lord, *let*

that sweet *voice of your word sound in my ears, by which you gave me hope:* Amen, I say to you, when the Son of Man sits on the throne of his majesty, you who have followed me in the regeneration will also sit on twelve thrones, judging.** *Ps 118:49 *Matt 19:28

But why does he say *in the regeneration*? What is this regeneration, brothers? We are not unaware that a person must be born again of water and the Holy Spirit.* *John 3:5 This hardly fits the regeneration mentioned here, however, so perhaps we must look for another regeneration, and must not only be born a second time but be reborn again, be born a third time. It is no wonder that this is so. In the first generation both parts of the human person were corrupted—the body by mortality and the soul by iniquity—while in the second generation, which is the first regeneration, only the soul is reformed; the body is not rid of its mortality, but the soul is rid of its iniquity. So another regeneration or resurrection is clearly needed, in which our bodies too will be restored, having been configured to the *body of* Christ's *glory*,* *Phil 3:21 provided our hearts have first been reformed to the gentleness and humility of the heart of Christ himself.* *Matt 11:29 *Happy* therefore *are they who have a share in the first resurrection*,* *Rev 20:6 because they will also share in the second.

4. *In* this *regeneration*, therefore, *when the Son of Man sits on the throne of his majesty, you will also sit and judge.** *Matt 19:28 This is what Scripture is referring to elsewhere when it says, *in exchange for their double shame and dishonor they will praise their lot.** *Isa 61:7 Two things accompany the poverty of those who follow the Lord: hardship and disparagement. The prophet speaks of these when he says, *see my humiliation and my toil.** *Ps 24:18 Because of them, *they will possess double in the land.** *Isa 61:7 In exchange for shame will be the honor of having the authority to judge. In exchange for toil will be the refreshment of sitting peacefully.

You who have followed me, he says, *when* I *sit you will also sit.** *Matt 19:28 It is as if he is saying, "You will join the one you follow provided you pursue him perseveringly; as

*Ps 33:15 it is written, *seek peace and pursue it*."* Therefore, I en-
1 Cor 9:24 treat you, dear brothers, run in such a way as to lay hold,
and refuse to sit down before you have clasped the
seated Christ and are worthy to be seated with him.
*Ps 18:6 *He exulted like a giant to run the course** the whole time
*Bar 3:38 *he was seen on earth and dwelt with humanity*,* and he did
not sit down until he had arrived at the point that he
had designated to be the end of his toil and sorrow
*Matt 26:38 when he said, *my soul is sorrowful even unto death*.* There-
*Matt 19:28 fore *when the Son of Man sits on the throne of majesty**—he
who had stood through the degrading punishment of
the cross as he was interrogated with insults and torture
Matt 19:28 in equal measure—you will also sit and judge, you
1 Pet 4:17 with whom the Judgment now begins and who give
Lam 2:18 yourselves but little rest, just as he himself came to be
John 12:47 judged and not to judge, *not to be served but to serve*.‡
‡Matt 20:28 *You will also sit*.† O, to sit! Who will grant me the gift
†Matt 19:28 to worthily express, brothers, what I foresee about this
sitting? Or rather, who will grant me the gift to experi-
ence the sweet, sweet rest of this sitting for which I long?
When will I sit, wretch that I am? At present neither
my body nor my soul sits; nothing in me is settled,
*Job 14:2 nothing is at rest, *nothing remains in the same state*.* *Un-*
*Rom 7:24 *happy man that I am! Who will deliver me** from the rest-
lessness of this inconstancy? My body is not allowed to
sit, prevented both by a sense of present pain and by a
dread of future death since it is mortal and able to suf-
**passibile est et mortale* fer.* My spirit has no rest either, on account of the
longing that belongs to hope and the anxiety provoked
by fear. When will that regeneration come when I will
be reborn to sit, miserable man that I am, who was born
Job 5:7 to toil?

It will surely come when the soul is partially at rest,
Ps 4:10 having been singularly settled in hope, and is free from
anxiety but not yet free from longing. I am talking
about after death but before the Day of Judgment. But
*Isa 14:3 *on that day*,* *when the Son of Man sits on the throne of his*

majesty,* we will sit perfectly and with every part. Neither the feeling of pain nor the fear of death will plague us. When our bodies have been glorified with a double robe of impassibility and immortality, we will also be free in our souls from all longing and all anxiety, lacking nothing, no longer fearing any danger, being completely secure and securely complete. *Matt 19:28

5. *You will sit,* says the Lord, says Truth itself, *you also will sit on twelve thrones judging the twelve tribes of Israel.** *Children of humanity, how long will your hearts be heavy? Why do you love what is futile and seek what is false?** *You seek glory from one another,** a glory that is vain and false—because *the children of humanity are vain; the children of humanity are liars**—*and you do not want the glory which comes from God alone,** the glory that unquestionably remains and is true, because he is the one who is,* and he is Truth.* We know that when he comes, *all will have their praise from God**—at least those who can now say *the taunts of your taunters fell on me** will have it. But you who are pitiful and pitiable,* following after vain glory, you cheat yourselves of true and eternal glory and do not deserve to be made sharers of it. You seek after transitory pleasure at whose entrance lies death,* and so you are never given to drink from the *torrent of* divine *delight,** nor are *you sated from its consoling breasts.*‡

*Matt 19:28
*Ps 4:3
*John 5:44
*Ps 61:10
*John 5:44
*Exod 3:14
*John 14:6
*1 Cor 4:5
*Rom 15:3
*_miseri et miserabiles_; see Rev 3:17
*RB 7.23
*Ps 35:9
‡Isa 66:11

But you say, "Yes, the divine promise is great, but the wait is too long." *Listen then, irksome house!** The waiting of this present time seems long to you? In fact you complain that a person's days are brief,* and you shrink with dread from the very toil that would have, by your own estimation, hastened your passing instead of adding to the length of your life. Besides, if it doesn't trouble you to toil for a single day in exchange for relaxing on the next day, a day that soon dies—although sometimes it might be better to call it deadly or deadening—why do you not much more willingly toil for forty years or more for the sake of everlasting rest and happiness? That

*Isa 7:13; Ezek 12:25
*Job 14:5

spiritual labor has an end is certain. Its reward is also certain, and what a reward it is! On the other hand, the length of these days is completely uncertain—if one should even speak of length when their shortness is confirmed so many times by the testimony of divine Scripture or, rather, is made clear to all by the ample evidence of those who die each day.

*Ps 102:14 What then? *The Lord knows of what we are made.**
**pusillanimitas* Because our faint-heartedness* cannot bear the delays of postponement, the Lord in his kindness addresses this thought of ours head-on and even answers it in part; for then he says, *and all who leave father or mother or children or lands for my sake will receive a hundred fold and*
*Matt 19:29 *will possess eternal life.**

*Ps 62:11 *The mouths of those who speak evil are silenced.* Let all*
*Ps 24:4 *who wantonly do wrong* now *be put to confusion.** For we
*1 Tim 4:8 have *the promise of life, of life now* as well as *of life to come.**
For it is clear that the promise of the hundredfold belongs to this present time since the words that follow
*Matt 19:29 it are *and they will possess eternal life.**

6. But to avoid leaving to the stubborn the slightest room for equivocation, I refer you to the gospel according to Mark, where it very openly declares that the promise of the hundredfold belongs to this present time. For the Lord says, *There is no one who has left father or mother or children or lands for my sake and for the sake of the Gospel who does not receive a hundred times as much*
*Mark 10:29-30 *now in this age, homes and brothers,** and everything else that follows. And *in order that you may be* even more
*John 5:20 *astounded,** and not think that this promise—even though it pertains to this present time—is offering tem-
*Mark 10:30 poral goods, it adds, *with persecutions.** After all, what earthly goods did the holy martyrs receive in the midst of their persecution, when even the very *earth* of their
*Job 9:24 bodies *was delivered into the hands of the wicked*?* Therefore, when it says, *a hundred times as much, houses or brothers,* and the rest, it can hardly be understood accord-

ing to the flesh. Obviously no one receives a hundred mothers! On the other hand, if we choose to understand the promise to refer to the sharing of possessions and the bonds of spiritual affection that exist between the elect, it could fit some of them, yes, but not all; for we know that some of the saints lacked this earthly and human consolation. It is within your heart and your inner being,* therefore, that you must search for this hundredfold, in order to have now, yes now, *the fruit that leads to your sanctification. But the end is eternal life.**

**homine interiori;* see Eph 3:16

*Rom 6:22

7. I am worried, however, that among those who appear to have left all things there may be some who would readily choose, if they dared, to murmur against this word and find it extremely hard to accept, and do so only because they feel pressured to by the authority of the Word itself, whose promises it is a sacrilege to doubt. I know full well that I would easily have found some challengers if I were saying these things on my own. As it is, however, even if some murmur, I speak with an untroubled conscience, because their *murmuring is not against us, but against the Lord,** against Truth, against him *in whose mouth is found no deceit.** He is the one who speaks to everyone alike; he rejects no one, excludes no one, but instead he says, *everyone who has left father or mother will receive a hundred fold,** and the rest. Or as the other Evangelist writes, *there is no one who has left father or mother who does not receive a hundred times as much now in this present time,** and the rest, as we said before.

*Exod 16:8

*1 Pet 2:22

*Matt 19:29

*Mark 10:29-30

Let those who have turned from the world but have not yet received the hundredfold go and search their hearts and carefully examine the conduct of their ways. They will undoubtedly discover there a nook or an inn that the Savior did not know;[2] it is *foxes* that *have a den*

[2] *angulum et diversorium quod Salvator non novit.* See also Bernard, Pur 1.2 and Asc 6.13 (SBOp 4:335; 5:158).

*Luke 9:58 *and birds of the air* that *have nests.** I implore them then to leave all things more perfectly. Let them *not seek what* *1 Cor 13:5 *is theirs.** Let them hold nothing back for themselves and nothing for others. Such is the case with some; although they disregard their own promotion and pleasure well enough, they in some way hold on to what they should relinquish for the sake of those who are close to them, working on their behalf with a fleshly solicitude that is wholly inconsistent with religious life. They are pitiful and pitiable people to be sure. As long *Mark 12:31 as they are not loving their neighbors as themselves,* they prove themselves unkind either to their neighbors or themselves, or, what is more true, to both.

Let them leave *all things*, therefore; let them follow Christ alone; let them strive to please Christ alone and cling with watchful solicitude to what is pleasing to his will. Without a doubt they will immediately experience what Truth promises to those who leave everything and follow him: *they will receive a hundred fold*, he says, *and will possess eternal life*. We receive the first along the way to console us, but the second we possess forever in the *beatitudinem homeland for our happiness.*

8. But what is this hundredfold, brothers? Is it not consolations, visitations, and the first fruits of the Spirit *Ps 18:11 who is *sweeter than honey*?* Is it not *the testimony of our* *2 Cor 1:12 *conscience*?* Is it not the glad and joyful *longing of the* *Prov 10:28 *just*?* Is it not *the memory of the abundance of* God's *sweet-* *Ps 30:20 *ness* as well as *the great wealth of sweetness* he *keeps hidden** *1 Cor 2:7, 9 for those who love him* that make it unnecessary to describe this sweetness to those who have already experienced it and impossible to describe to those who have not? It is not father or mother, home or field, food or clothing. Ultimately, it is not anything earthly or physical, but it is clearly something that is much more delightful than all of these, sweeter than every one of them, more blissful than them all—and nothing that we desire in this wicked world can be compared to it.

The generous gift of this grace—the consolation of this present life and the rewards yet to be gained—he deigns to bestow on us in his abundant kindness, he who came so that we might have life and have it more abundantly,* Jesus Christ our Lord, *who is over all, God blessed forever, Amen.**

*John 10:10

*Rom 9:5

Appendix

The Life of Saint Victor by an Unknown but Ancient Author[1]

Chapter 1: The birth, education, priesthood, and anchoretic life of Saint Victor and the wine obtained by his prayers.

1. The splendor of the Lord has shone forth on* the just, whose fame rolls unceasingly round the earth. We are not speaking here of those possessed of prodigious power, but of those who are seen to serve Christ with a docile mind, with devoted faith. When Job, that holiest of men, contended with the ancient enemy of the human race, he was plagued with dreadful sores from the tip of his head to the soles of his feet and afflicted with worms,* but he won the Lord's grace by his patience. Was he put to the test because God did not know whether or not he was just? Certainly not, but so that having been proved he might be justified, and so that everyone might know that it is possible for a human being to overcome the devil with the Lord's help. The battle's struggle is great, and it is only by Christ's victory that we are triumphant.

*See Ps 89:17

*Job 2:7; 7:5

2. There was a victor who had the joy of having that sweet name of Victor as his own, sprung from a glorious lineage in the diocese of Troyes. He got his name before he received his limbs, before his pregnant mother released him from his waiting. When a certain man was racked by an unclean spirit,* the man cried out saying, "Why do you torment us before you even begin to be born, holy victor of God?"* We are not looking here to the demons for their testimony, however, but for their confession. They proclaimed by name *the truth that later events would prove.**

*Luke 6:18

*See Matt 8:29

*Gen 41:13

[1] *Acta Sanctorum Bollandia*, Feb. III (Paris, 1865), 671–72.

Then, seven months later, at the beginning of her tenth month, the mother's inner members were moved, and she brought forth the holy offspring, the godly* Victor, into the world. After the set number of days had passed, he was bathed in the baptismal waters and cleansed by heavenly grace from original sin. When he was placed in his cradle his parents looked and were struck with amazement to see the Holy Spirit resting on the tiny baby.* But this was only a foreshadowing of what would afterwards be fulfilled in him. The child grew in body, but even while clothed in childish infancy he had a mind that was mature in the Lord.

**pium*

*See Luke 3:22

3. He was first filled with instruction by a dedication to the study of letters, while, being devoted to fasting and prayer, he continually gave away his meals as alms for the poor. Then, leaving behind his worldly studies, he became emptied for divine reading. He preached the words of the Scriptures and the sweetness of the Christian faith to the acclaim of the people, and brimmed with those words David sang: *How sweet are your words to my mouth, Lord. They are honey and honeycomb upon my lips.** When he reached the legal age he received the responsibility of the clerical state in the regular way, then ascended to the office of deacon, and eventually to the rank of the priestly order. Not long afterwards, he left his parents and moved to the Arcies region, and there in a village called Saturniac he was loved by all the inhabitants of that place and its illustrious men on account of the grace of Christ in him. There, secluded in a cell day and night, he devoted himself unceasingly to fasting and to prayer, praying for pardon for the people and for the forgiveness of sins.

*Ps 118:103

4. While Victor was living there, one of the Frankish kings came roaming the countryside on a hunt, leading his horses along the shady riverbanks and taking his hawks to the most beautiful spots.* Hearing of the blessed man's reputation, the king was filled with joy

**aemonissima loca*

and approached his hut, but nothing was hidden from the blessed man, and he quickly came out of his cell to meet him. When the king saw Victor, he ran to meet him and kissed him. Then the venerable man began by saying, "If the high dignity of your kingly office has no objection, do the honor of entering your servant's hut." When the king had come inside, Victor said to one of the boys, "Bring me the small vessel that is normally used to carry wine."

When the boy had brought it, Victor prostrated himself in prayer, pouring out these petitions to the Lord: "God, you whose throne is on high and whose power surpasses all; who hung the heavens above the earth and adorned them with a variety of stars as with beautiful gems; who commanded me to come into this world from my mother's womb and to confess your holy name, bless this vessel and fill it with heavenly dew, so that just as our fathers were satisfied with manna in the desert, so we may be filled with the gift of your blessing." As Victor made the sign of the cross, immediately the vessel was filled with the wine of gladness, whose sweetness is *sweeter than honey** and which no tongue *Ps 18:11
can describe. Drinking it, the whole crowd was satisfied and everyone set out on their way leaping with joy. The kindness of the one who turned water into wine at Cana of Galilee* was not lacking in that place, and what *John 2:1-11
was not wine by nature, what had not hung or come forth from the vine, was changed into Falernian wine at Christ's word.

5. There is a particular miracle that should not be kept silent, but which must be told. One day Victor sent workers into the field to sow wheat, and one of them dug and fashioned a hole in the ground that could hold two measures. Immediately the man was convulsed by a demon, as if seized by a lion, and belched forth flames from both sides of his mouth. The man of God, seeing him from afar, made the sign of the cross and cleansed him, and the wheat that the man had hidden was restored to its rightful hands.

Chapter 2: Saint Victor's Heavenly Visions, his Death, and his Miracles.

6. One day when he was resting his body, weakened by hunger from fasting and prayer, Victor rose in the dark silence of the night and prostrated himself in a certain place to pray for the world. When he got up he saw *the heavens opened** and the Lord's cross glittering with a golden splendor, each part adorned with precious stones, and he heard a voice saying to him, "Those jewels that you see are the souls of the saints who for the sake of Christ the Lord washed *their robes in the blood of the lamb*."* Struck with fear, Victor fell upon his face, magnifying the Lord, who laid open earthly secrets to him. From that day on he remained hidden away, enclosed in his cell, and although he no longer went out into the world to make himself available to the laity, many afflicted people of many different languages still came to him and were healed.

*Acts 7:55

*Rev 7:14; 22:14

7. There is another mystery I do not think should be left untold but should be proclaimed for the sake of the real virtue there is in praising so great a man. When this blessed man grew very old, shunning everything worldly and scorning those transitory things that the world considers delightful, his gray hair had earned respect, and he was perfect in charity. In the midst of worldly nobility he was divinely favored, being especially loved by all. During that time, this honorable man had a spiritual son in a village named Cupidiniac, who belonged to another race of the Franks and whom Victor had received from the waters of the sacred font. This man strenuously implored Victor to do him the favor of visiting his house and family, since he had been longing for him to come for such a long time. The blessed man did not refuse, promised a day, and did what he had pledged to do. When he came to the house, everyone met him with joy and received him as if he were a heavenly gift or a gleaming pearl. He took no food except when the day was already drawing towards evening, and after eating he gave himself, or rather his tiny body, over to rest for a little while.

One night during this visit, rising in the middle of the night as was his custom, he invoked the Lord with psalms and hymns in sweet song until the dawn grew bright and shed its light upon the Lord's day. When he had finished solemn Matins, he went to be with the crowds of people and taught them about the Catholic religion. As his sermon grew long and the hour drew near, the people hurried to church to hear the sacred mysteries, as was the custom. They say that Victor remained behind in a certain spot, and there he heard the company of angels completing the Lord's prayer where it says, *but deliver us from evil.** Stunned, with his head *Matt 6:13
bowed to the earth, striking his chest with both of his hands at the same time, he said, "Woe is me, for I am unworthy, Lord Jesus, to deserve to hear with my own ears the angels' indescribable voices praying the prayer you yourself taught your disciples to say." Then he said, "Let us return home since the divine services have already been offered in heaven." Victor was not puffed up with human conceit when he heard the angels, but instead marveled at the goodness of God at work, because the Lord loves those who worship him, and *does not forsake all who hope in him.** Nevertheless, they re- *Ps 33:23
mained there the rest of that day, eating and drinking in equal measure, and on the following day Victor returned to his cell in joy, leaving everyone in good stead.

8. I have recounted just a few of the many things that could be said about this man, lest I weary my readers. According to the people's testimony, Victor also restored sight to the blind, hearing to the deaf, and speech to the mute, and made the lame to walk. On the fourth of March he went to the Lord and was buried in a lovely

*loco amoeno

spot.* There his holy limbs are held in a grave while his spirit seeks the stars[2] in great triumph.

9. It happened that at that time there was a man who had committed the sin of theft, been apprehended in a field of Arcies, locked up in the custody of prison guards, and was being held prisoner for a long time. In a vision he saw the Blessed Victor, who seemed with his staff to touch the clasp of the chains that bound him. When the man awoke he saw that he had been granted a miracle, because the chains that had held him fast had fallen from his hands and neck and now remained only on his feet. He was nervous about how to act or what to do, but, coming to his senses, he decided to seek refuge at the church[3] of the holy man, and as chance would have it, the chains fell from his feet. With the prison guard sprawled lifeless on the ground, seized by the deep sleep of the Lord, the one who had been chained got up and attempted to see if he could walk. His legs wobbled as he tried to direct his stride. The prison door lay open, and he held a snatched spear in his hands. At first he could barely walk, bent over as he was, but his spirit grew stronger and stronger and his health returned. There could be no obstacle for the one whom divine power had rescued. He made such a swift course through the silence of that dark night that he ran six thousand paces as if he had not walked a single furlong,[4] and it seemed to him as if he enjoyed the help of an angel's hand. For when he entered the churchyard and reached the doors of the church, immediately the iron cuff broke and shattered into many pieces, leaving him holding in his hands the broken remains of what had once shackled

[2] *spiritus astra petit*. These words are traditionally attributed to Ovid.

[3] *basilica* often refers to a church built over the tomb of a saint.

[4] *unum stadium*, or one furlong, equals 125 paces.

his feet, showing it to the people who were there witnessing these events. Yes, the kindness of our Savior has deigned to produce many signs and wonders through Victor at his tomb, even to the present day, as our Lord Jesus Christ reigns, to whom be honor and glory for all ages. Amen.

Scriptural Index

Scriptural references are identified by sermon and paragraph number or by VSV (the Life of Saint Victor) and paragraph number.

Subject Index

Entries are cited by sermons and paragraphs, with T indicating a sermon title and n. a note number within a sermon. VSV is the *Life of Saint Victor*. Some words are identified as adjectives, nouns, or verbs, abbreviated *a*, *n*, or *v*.